J.K. LASSER'S™

NEW
TAX LAW
SIMPLIFIED

Look for these and other titles from J.K. Lasser™—Practical Guides for All Your Financial Needs

J.K. Lasser's Pick Winning Stocks
by Edward F. Mrkvicka, Jr.

J.K. Lasser's Invest Online
by LauraMaery Gold and Dan Post

J.K. Lasser's Year-Round Tax Strategies
by David S. DeJong and Ann Gray Jakabcin

J.K. Lasser's Taxes Made Easy for Your Home-Based Business
by Gary W. Carter

J.K. Lasser's Finance and Tax for Your Family Business
by Barbara Weltman

J.K. Lasser's Pick Winning Mutual Funds
by Jerry Tweddell with Jack Pierce

J.K. Lasser's Your Winning Retirement Plan
by Henry K. Hebeler

J.K. Lasser's Winning with Your 401(k)
by Grace Weinstein

J.K. Lasser's Winning with Your 403(b)
by Pam Horowitz

J.K. Lasser's Strategic Investing after 50
by Julie Jason

J.K. Lasser's Winning Financial Strategies for Women
by Rhonda Ecker and Denise Gustin-Piazza

J.K. Lasser's Pick Stocks Like Warren Buffett
by Warren Boroson

J.K. Lasser's New Tax Law Simplified

J.K. LASSER'S™

NEW TAX LAW SIMPLIFIED

John Wiley & Sons, Inc.

New York • Chichester • Weinheim • Brisbane • Singapore • Toronto

ISBN: 0-471-09280-0

Printed in the United States of America.

10 9 8 7 6 5 4 3 2 1

Contents

Introduction   **1**

1. Income Tax Rate Reductions   **21**

Individual Income Tax Structure   21

   Tax Rates for 2001 under the New Law   24

   Rebate Checks   29

Repeal of Phaseout of Itemized Deductions   30

Repeal of Phaseout of Personal Exemptions   33

Alternative Minimum Tax Relief   36

2. Tax Relief for Families   **39**

Tax Benefits Relating to Children   39

   Increase and Expansion of Child Tax Credit   39

   Extension and Expansion of Adoption

      Tax Benefits   42

   Expansion of Dependent Care Tax Credit   46

Marriage Penalty Relief 49
  Standard Deduction Marriage Penalty Relief 50
  Expansion of the 15 Percent Rate Bracket
    for Married Couples Filing Joint Returns 51
  Marriage Penalty Relief and Simplification
    Relating to the Earned Income Credit 53
  Sale of Principal Residence—In Conjunction
    with Estate Tax Changes 60

3. Tax Relief for Educational Expenses **61**
Education IRAs 62
Section 529 Qualified Tuition Plans 66
College Education Deductions 70
Educational Assistance Plans 74
Coordination of the Education Incentives 75
  Education IRAs and Education Credits 77
  Contributions to Education IRAs and
    Qualified Tuition Plans 78
  Qualified Tuition Programs, Education IRAs,
    and Education Credits 78
  College Tuition Education Deductions 79
  Coverage by Educational Assistance Plans 79
Student Loans 80
Scholarships under the National Health
  Service Corps and the Armed Forces
  Health Professions Programs 82

**4. Estate, Gift, and Generation-Skipping Transfer
Tax Relief** **85**
Phaseout and Repeal of the Estate Tax and
  Generation-Skipping Tax; Modification of
  the Gift Tax 86

Reduction in State Death Tax Credit;
    Deduction for State Death Taxes Paid   91
Basis of Property Acquired from Decedent   92
Basis Increase for Certain Property   96
Income Tax Exclusion for the Gain on the
    Sale of a Principal Residence   100
Reporting Requirements   102
Installment Payment of Estate Tax for Closely
    Held Businesses   104
Transfers to Foreign Trusts, Foreign
    Estates, and Nonresidents Who Are Not
    U.S. Citizens   107
Transfers of Property in Satisfaction of
    Pecuniary Bequest   109
Expansion of Estate Tax Rule for
    Conservation Easements   110
Generation-Skipping Transfer Tax Rules   113

5. Pension and Individual Retirement
   Arrangement Relief   **115**
Individual Retirement Arrangements   115
Qualified Plan Contributions and Benefits   121
    Increase in Benefit and Contribution Limits   121
    Compensation Limit   123
    Elective Deferral Limitations   124
    Option to Treat Elective Deferrals as Roth
      Contributions   126
    Nonrefundable Credit to Certain
      Individuals for Elective Deferrals and
      IRA Contributions   128
    Additional Deferrals for Employees Age
      50 or Older   131

Faster Vesting of Employer Matching
Contributions 134
Modifications to Minimum Distribution
Rules 136
457 Plans 137
Provisions Relating to Hardship Withdrawals 142
Pension Coverage for Domestic and
Similar Workers 144
Increasing Portability for Participants 145
Rollovers of Retirement Plan and
IRA Distributions 145
Waiver of 60-Day Rule 147
Automatic Rollovers of Certain Mandatory
Distributions 149
Explanation of Tax Consequences for
Recipients of Rollover Distributions 150
Treatment of Forms of Distribution 151
Business Owners and Plan Administration 155
Notice of Significant Reduction in Plan Benefit 155
Deduction Limits 157
Plan Loans for S Corporation Shareholders,
Partners, and Sole Proprietors 158
Modification of Top-Heavy Rules 159
Elective Deferrals Not Taken into Account
for Purposes of Deduction Limits 163
Repeal of Coordination Requirements for
Deferred Compensation Plans of State
and Local Governments and
Tax-Exempt Organizations 164
Elimination of IRS User Fees for Certain
Determination Letter Requests
Regarding Employer Plans 166

Small Business Tax Credit for New
  Retirement Plan Expenses   168
Contributions of Employees to Defined
  Contribution Plans   169
Distributions after Separation from Service   170
Employers May Disregard Rollovers for
  Purposes of Cash-Out Rules   173
Investment of Employee Contributions
  in 401(k) Plans   174
Treatment of Employer-Provided
  Retirement Advice   176

Appendix   **179**

Glossary   **221**

Index   **251**

Introduction

Many Tax Breaks under the New Law Are Delayed or Uncertain

Apart from delivery of a rebate check this summer or fall, the new tax law will not have much immediate impact. Although the Economic Growth and Tax Relief Reconciliation Act of 2001 provides the most sweeping tax cut in 20 years, budgetary constraints and political compromises resulted in a crazy quilt of phase-ins and temporary benefits. Some benefits are delayed for years while others last for only a few years before they expire. Future Congresses may reverse scheduled tax breaks before they ever take effect, while expiring benefits will have to be extended or they will disappear. **In fact, to comply with budget reconciliation rules, the entire Act will automatically termi-**

nate, or "sunset," at the end of 2010 unless Congress extends the provisions. If the law sunsets, the pre-Act rules would apply as if the Act had never become law.

If the phase-ins take effect and expiring provisions are extended, significant tax relief may be realized in the form of tax rate reductions, expanded retirement plan benefits, increased child credits, educational tax breaks, marriage penalty relief, and phaseout of the estate tax. However, critics warn that the income tax reductions promised by the Act will not be realized by millions of taxpayers who are expected to become subject to the alternative minimum tax (AMT), which was inadequately addressed by the Act. The need to focus on the growing AMT problem as well as the Act's scheduled sunset after 2010 guarantees that the new law provisions will have to be revisited by Congress.

Summary of Major Provisions

Rebate Checks or Credit for 2001

The Treasury Department began mailing out rebate checks at the end of July to individuals who reported tax liability on their 2000 tax returns (after nonrefundable tax credits). First-time filers and those who did not have any 2000 tax liability may receive a tax credit on their 2001 returns instead of the rebate check. Dependents are not eligible for the check or the credit.

The rebate checks represent an advance payment of the tax savings from the creation of the new 10 percent tax bracket for 2001. The 10 percent bracket applies to the first $12,000 of taxable income for married couples filing jointly and qualified widow(er)s, the first $10,000 for a head of household, and the first $6,000 for a single taxpayer or married person filing separately. These amounts would have been taxed at 15 percent under prior law. Instead of using withholding changes or making taxpayers wait until they file for 2001 to get the benefit of the 10 percent rate, Congress decided on the rebate checks, to be calculated based on 2000 filing information, in the hope that this approach would help stimulate the economy.

The amount of the check will be 5 percent (the difference between the 10 percent and 15 percent rates) of the first $12,000, $10,000, or $6,000 of taxable income for 2000, depending on filing status. A married couple filing jointly for 2000 or a qualified widow(er) will receive a $600 rebate check if taxable income was at least $12,000. For head of household filers with 2000 taxable income of $10,000 or more, the rebate check will be $500. The rebate check will be $300 for a filer who is single or married filing separately with taxable income of at least $6,000. If the tax liability for 2000 was less than the maximum rebate ($300, $500, or $600), the payment is limited to the smaller of the liability or 5% of taxable income for 2000.

Checks will be mailed in weekly batches starting at the end of July with taxpayers whose Social Security numbers end with "00." You should receive your rebate check by the end of September if you filed your 2000 return by April 16. If you filed later, with or without a filing extension, the check will be sent by the end of the year.

Individuals who did not have tax liability for 2000 but owe tax for 2001 will not receive a check, but may be able to claim a 5 percent credit on their 2001 returns. The credit will be figured on a worksheet in the 2001 instructions, subject to the same limit as the rebate checks. If a rebate check is received for 2000 for an amount that is less than the credit based on 2001 taxable income and tax liability, the difference is allowed as a tax credit on the return for 2001. This could happen where taxable income for 2000 was under the $12,000, $10,000, or $6,000 limit for rebate check purposes, but taxable income for 2001 is at least that much. If the rebate check is larger than the credit due based on 2001 taxable income, the difference does not have to be repaid to the Treasury.

The rebate checks and the tax credit are the mechanisms by which the new 10 percent bracket is being implemented for 2001. After 2001, the 10 percent bracket will be reflected in the IRS tax tables and rate schedules, and taken into account for wage withholding purposes.

Small Tax Rate Reductions for 2001

In addition to the rebate check or credit just discussed, each tax bracket over 15 percent is reduced by 1 percent effective July 1, 2001, resulting in a 0.5 percent reduction for 2001. For example, the 2001 28 percent bracket is reduced to 27.5 percent and the 31 percent, 36 percent, and 39.6 percent brackets are also lowered by half a percent. The IRS has provided employers with revised wage withholding tables that reflect the change.

Phased-in Tax Rate Reductions Starting in 2002

After 2001, there will be six tax brackets. The 10 percent and 15 percent rates will not be reduced. Reductions to rates over 15 percent will be completely phased in by 2006 (for a greater discussion see Chapter 1, "Income Tax Rate Reductions"). Although the amount of taxable income within each rate bracket generally changes annually, the 10 percent bracket will apply through 2007 to taxable income up to $12,000 (joint returns), $10,000 (head of household), or $6,000 (single). In 2008, the first $7,000 of taxable income for single filers and the first $14,000 for joint filers will be subject to the 10 percent rate. For married couples filing jointly, the 15 percent bracket will be expanded between 2005 and 2008; see the discussion of marriage penalty relief in Chapter 2, "Tax Relief for Families."

Child Tax Credit Liberalized This Year

The tax credit for each child under age 17 increases from $500 to $600 for 2001. The income eligibility rules for the credit have not been changed.

The credit will remain at $600 per eligible child through 2004, increasing to $700 for 2005 through 2008, to $800 in 2009, and to $1,000 for 2010 and later years.

The credit has been made partly refundable. If the allowable credit exceeds regular tax and alternative minimum tax (AMT) liability, a refund will be allowed on a 2001 return to the extent of 10 percent of earned income in excess of $10,000. After 2001, the $10,000 earnings floor may be increased by an inflation factor. In 2005, the refundable percentage increases to 15 percent.

The prior-law rule that allowed the child credit for 2000 and 2001 to offset regular tax liability plus any AMT is permanently extended beyond 2001.

Minimal AMT Relief

Despite the consensus that millions of taxpayers will not benefit from the Act's income tax reductions if they become subject to the alternative minimum tax (AMT), the new law provides minimal relief that lasts for only four years.

The AMT exemption increases to $49,000 from $45,000 for married couples filing jointly and qualified widow(er)s. For single filers and heads of household, the exemption increases to $35,750 from $33,750. For married persons filing separately, the increase is to $24,500 from $22,500. This limited relief applies only for 2001 through 2004; the AMT reform buck has been passed to future Congresses, who presumably will be forced to address the issue over the next few years.

The new law allows the AMT to be offset by the child tax credit and the adoption credit and provides that the refundable earned income credit and the additional child credit for families with three or more children are not reduced by AMT liability.

Itemized Deduction and Personal Exemption Restrictions

Higher-income taxpayers will receive an extra tax cut between 2006 and 2010, when the 3 percent reduction to itemized deductions and the phaseout of personal exemptions are eliminated. Both restrictions will be reduced by one-third in 2006 and 2007, reduced by two-thirds in 2008 and 2009, and completely eliminated starting in 2010.

Marriage Penalty Relief Delayed

Although marriage penalty relief for couples filing jointly was one of the pillars of the original Bush tax-cut plan, the new law delays reforms until 2005 and then phases them in over four or five years. Many joint filers will not be affected by the changes.

Married couples who file jointly and claim the standard deduction instead of itemizing will be entitled to a slightly higher deduction after 2004. The standard deduction on joint returns, now 167 percent of the standard deduction for single taxpayers ($7,600 compared to $4,550), will be 174 percent of the deduction for singles in 2005, 184 percent in 2006, 187 percent in 2007, 190 percent in 2008, and finally twice as much in 2009 and later.

Starting in 2005, an expansion of the 15 percent bracket will ease marriage penalties for joint filers with taxable incomes near the upper limit of the bracket. The end point of the 15 percent bracket for joint returns, now 167 percent of the end point for single returns ($45,200 compared to $27,050), will increase to 180 percent of the end point for singles in 2005, 187 percent in 2006, 193 percent in 2007, and 200 percent in 2008 and thereafter.

For joint filers eligible for the earned income credit, the income phaseout range for the credit will start and end $1,000 later than for unmarried taxpayers in the years 2002 to 2004, $2,000 more in 2005 to 2007, and $3,000 more in 2008, with the $3,000 increase subject to inflation adjustments.

Dependent Care Credit

The dependent care credit will be expanded starting in 2003. A maximum of $3,000 of employment-related expenses for one dependent and $6,000 for more than one dependent will be eligible for the credit, up from $2,400 and

$4,800, respectively. The maximum credit percentage increases to 35 percent (from 30 percent) for taxpayers with adjusted gross income (AGI) of $15,000 or less (up from $10,000), phasing down to a minimum credit of 20 percent for taxpayers with AGI over $43,000. Under current law, the minimum 20 percent credit applies to those with AGI over $28,000.

EMPLOYER CREDIT FOR DEPENDENT CARE FACILITIES. Starting in 2002, employers may claim a tax credit for 25 percent of the costs of buying, building, rehabilitating, or operating a child care facility. A 10 percent credit will be allowed for child care resource and referral services. The combined credit may not exceed $150,000 per year.

Adoption Credit and Employee Exclusion

The adoption credit for children without special needs, scheduled to expire at the end of 2001, has been permanently extended. For 2002, the maximum credit per eligible child (whether or not with special needs) is increased to $10,000, up from $6,000 for special needs adoptions and $5,000 for other adoptions. More taxpayers will qualify for the credit, as the $40,000 income phaseout will start at $150,000 instead of $75,000 for all eligible adoptions. For all years after 2001, the credit offsets AMT liability. After 2001, the credit for special needs adoptions is allowed only in the year the adoption is finalized.

The exclusion for employer-provided adoption assistance is extended beyond 2001, subject to the same $10,000 limit and $150,000 phaseout threshold as the credit. These amounts may be adjusted for inflation after 2002.

Starting in 2003, a $10,000 credit or employee exclusion is allowed for a special needs adoption in the year the adoption is finalized even if the taxpayer's qualified adoption expenses are less than $10,000.

IRAs and Employer Retirement Plans

TRADITIONAL IRA AND ROTH IRA CONTRIBUTIONS. The $2,000 contribution limit for individual retirement accounts (IRAs), deductible for traditional IRAs and nondeductible for Roth IRAs, is increasing to $3,000 for 2002 to 2004, $4,000 for 2005 to 2007, and $5,000 for 2008. After 2008, the $5,000 limit will be subject to inflation adjustments. The $2,000 deductible limit for traditional IRAs had been in effect since 1981.

For individuals age 50 or over as of the end of the year, contribution limits are raised still further: The annual limit is increased by $500 for 2002 to 2005 and by $1,000 for 2006 and later years. For example, an individual who is at least age 50 in 2002 may contribute $3,500 to a Roth IRA if not barred by the phaseout rules.

The phaseout rules, based on modified adjusted gross income (MAGI), were not changed by the new law and will prevent some individuals from taking advantage of the higher contribution limits. For example, the $3,000 Roth IRA contribution limit ($3,500 if age 50 or older) for 2002 will be phased out for single individuals with MAGI between $95,000 and $110,000 and for married persons filing jointly with MAGI between $150,000 and $160,000. The $3,000 deductible traditional IRA limit for 2002 ($3,500 if age 50 or over) will be phased out for a single individual who is an active participant in an employer retirement plan if MAGI is between $34,000 and $44,000. For a married active participant who files jointly, the phaseout range is $54,000 to $64,000 for 2002.

ELECTIVE DEFERRALS TO 401(K), 403(B), SEP, SIMPLE, AND 457 PLANS. The limits on elective deferrals to employer retirement plans are being increased starting in 2002. However, the higher contribution amounts will be available only if they are permitted under the terms of the plan. In addition, they are subject to nondiscrimination rules that may require lower deferral limits for highly compensated employees. Plan participants who are age 50 or older are allowed to increase the applicable contribution limit by an additional amount, as discussed next.

The current elective deferral limit of $10,500 for 401(k), 403(b), and salary-reduction simplified employee pension (SEP) plans is increasing to $11,000 in 2002 and then by $1,000 in each of the next four years until it reaches $15,000 in 2006. Starting in 2007, the $15,000 limit may be increased for inflation.

The elective deferral limit for SIMPLE plans, now $6,500, increases to $7,000 for 2002 and then increases by $1,000 a year until it reaches $10,000 in 2005. In later years, the $10,000 limit may be eligible for inflation adjustments.

The elective deferral limit for 457 plans (state and local governments and tax-exempt organizations), currently $8,500, will follow the 401(k) plan limits, increasing to $11,000 for 2002 and to $15,000 by 2006. The dollar limit is doubled in the three years prior to retirement. The applicable dollar limit applies as long as it does not exceed 100 percent of the participant's compensation; prior law set a limit of $33\frac{1}{3}$ percent of compensation.

Plan participants who are age 50 or older by the end of the year may contribute more than the aforementioned limits if the additional contributions are available on an equal basis to all participants meeting the age test. For 2002, an additional $1,000 may be contributed to a 401(k), 403(b), SEP, or 457 plan. Thus, if permitted by the plan, a participant age 50 or older may make an elective deferral of up to $12,000 for 2002 (the $11,000 regular limit increased by $1,000). The extra contribution increases to $2,000 in 2003, $3,000 in 2004, $4,000 in 2005, and $5,000 in 2006. For a SIMPLE plan, the additional contribution is half as much: $500 for 2002, $1,000 for 2003, $1,500 for 2004, $2,000 for 2005, and $2,500 for 2006. After 2006, the additional contribution limits of $5,000 for 401(k), 403(b), SEP, and 457 plans and $2,500 for SIMPLE plans are subject to inflation adjustments.

OPTIONAL ROTH 401(K) OR 403(B) AFTER 2005. For tax years starting after 2005, a 401(k) or 403(b) plan may permit participants to treat elective deferrals as after-tax Roth contributions held in a separate account, instead of receiving regular pre-tax treatment. As with a Roth IRA, tax-free distributions could be received after a five-year waiting period by participants over age $59\frac{1}{2}$.

DEFINED CONTRIBUTION PLAN AND PENSION PLAN CONTRIBUTIONS. Highly compensated individuals may benefit from increased qualified plan contribution and benefit limits. For years starting after 2001, the current $35,000 limit for total contributions (employee and employer plus forfeitures) to a participant's defined contribution plan account increases to $40,000. The limit on benefits from a defined benefit pension plan increases to $160,000 from $140,000 for years ending after 2001.

Employers will be able to deduct profit sharing plan or stock bonus plan contributions up to 25 percent of a participant's compensation for years starting after 2001; the prior-law limit was 15 percent. Compensation of up to $200,000 (increased from $170,000) may be taken into account.

The $40,000, $160,000, and $200,000 limits are subject to inflation adjustments.

RETIREMENT SAVINGS TAX CREDIT FOR LOWER-INCOME WORKERS. A tax credit will be allowed from 2002 to 2006 to encourage retirement contributions by low-to-moderate-income taxpayers. The credit applies to contributions to Roth or traditional IRAs and to 401(k), 403(b), 457, SIMPLE, or SEP plans. Depending on income, a credit of 10 percent, 20 percent, or 50 percent may be allowed for contributions up to $2,000. No credit is allowed to married persons filing jointly with MAGI over $50,000, heads of household with MAGI over $37,500, and all others with MAGI over $25,000. Dependents, full-time students, and workers under age 18 are not eligible for the credit.

EMPLOYER CREDIT FOR START-UP COSTS. Small business employers who set up a new qualified retirement plan, SIMPLE, or SEP after 2001 may claim a tax credit of up to $500 (50 percent of the first $1,000 of expenses) for administrative and retirement education costs for the first three years of the plan. The plan must cover at least one non–highly compensated employee to qualify.

FASTER VESTING OF MATCHING CONTRIBUTIONS. For plan years starting after 2001, either employees must be 100 percent vested in employer matching contributions after three years of service or the contributions must vest 20 percent per year starting with the second year of service until 100 percent is vested after the sixth year. Under prior law, the alternative vesting schedules did not require 100 percent vesting until after the fifth and seventh years.

GREATER ROLLOVER OPPORTUNITIES. Any rollover-eligible distribution after 2001 from a traditional IRA, qualified employer plan, 403(b) plan, or 457 plan may be rolled over to any of such plans, assuming the plan accepts rollovers. An employee's after-tax contributions may be rolled over to a qualified plan or traditional IRA.

For distributions after 2001, the Internal Revenue Service (IRS) has been given discretion to waive on equitable grounds the 60-day deadline for completing a rollover. Waiver is appropriate where failure to complete the rollover within 60 days is due to health reasons, errors made by a financial institution, natural disaster, or other events beyond the control of the individual.

Education Tax Breaks

EDUCATION IRAS. For 2002 and later years, the maximum contribution to an Education IRA will jump from $500 to $2,000, and contributions may be made until April 15 of the following year, as with traditional and Roth IRAs.

The contribution phaseout range for married persons filing jointly, now $150,000 to $160,000 of MAGI, will increase to $190,000 to $220,000, double the single filer's range.

In a major expansion, tax-free distributions from Education IRAs may be made after 2001 to cover qualified elementary and secondary private and religious school costs, as well as higher education expenses.

Claiming tax-free treatment for an Education IRA distribution will no longer bar a Hope or Lifetime Learning tuition credit in the same year for the same student so long as the credit and the exclusion cover different expenses.

SECTION 529 QUALIFIED TUITION PLANS. Distributions from state-sponsored tuition plans in 2002 will be fully excluded from gross income to the extent they cover qualified higher education costs. For 2001 and prior years, distributions allocable to earnings on the contract are taxable.

Starting in 2002, private colleges and universities may sponsor qualified prepaid tuition programs through an IRS-approved trust; savings plans are not allowed. Tax-free distributions from qualifying private prepaid programs will be allowed after 2003.

EMPLOYER-PROVIDED ASSISTANCE. The $5,250 exclusion for employer-provided education assistance, set to expire at the end of 2001, will be made permanent and expanded to include graduate-level courses starting in 2002.

STUDENT LOAN INTEREST DEDUCTION. The new law increases income eligibility for the student loan interest deduction and eliminates the 60-month limitation on the deduction. For 2002, the MAGI phaseout range for single taxpayers is $50,000 to $65,000, up from $40,000 to $55,000. On joint returns, the phaseout range increases to $100,000 to $130,000, up from $60,000 to $75,000. After 2002, the phaseout ranges will be indexed for inflation.

The deduction will no longer be limited to the first 60 months in which interest payments are required, effective for interest paid after 2001. Voluntary payments of interest during a period of loan forbearance will also be deductible.

NEW COLLEGE TUITION DEDUCTION. An above-the-line deduction (whether or not you itemize) for college tuition and related fees is available in 2002 through 2005 if income does not exceed a specified limit. The deduction is an alternative to a Hope or Lifetime Learning credit; both a deduction and credit may not be claimed for the same student in the same year.

In 2002 and 2003, up to $3,000 of qualifying expenses will be deductible for single filers with MAGI up to $65,000 and for married persons filing jointly with MAGI up to $130,000. For 2004 and 2005, the maximum deduction will rise to $4,000. A reduced deduction limit of $2,000 will apply in 2004 and 2005 to single filers with MAGI between $65,000 and $80,000, and married persons filing jointly with MAGI over $130,000 but not over $160,000.

Estate Tax Phased Out

Starting in 2002, the current unified tax system for taxable gifts and estate tax will change. The estate tax will be gradually reduced until it is repealed in 2010. The gift tax will not be repealed, but a $1 million lifetime exclusion will be allowed after 2001, and gift tax rates will gradually decline. A modified carryover basis system will take effect for inherited assets when the estate tax is repealed.

Estate and gift tax planning in light of these major changes is made more complicated by the long phaseout of the estate tax and the uncertainty created by the scheduled sunset of the 2001 Tax Relief Act at the end of 2010. The repeal of the estate tax will apply only for 2010 and the pre-Act rates and exemption will then return unless Congress extends the Act provisions.

STEPPED-UP BASIS FOR INHERITED PROPERTY LIMITED AFTER 2009. Until 2010, inherited property will continue to receive a basis stepped up to the fair market value of the asset on the date of death. The step-up in basis will be limited starting in 2010 when the estate tax is repealed. Generally, the basis for inherited property will be the decedent's basis where that is less than the date-of-death value, but there are two key exceptions. An executor will be allowed to increase the basis of inherited assets by up to a total of $1.3 million. The basis of property transferred to a surviving spouse could be increased by an additional $3 million, for a potential total basis increase of $4.3 million for a surviving spouse. Numerous details and exceptions complicate the carryover basis provisions.

FAMILY-OWNED BUSINESS DEDUCTION REPEALED. The deduction is repealed for estates of individuals dying after 2003.

STATE DEATH TAX CREDIT PHASED OUT. The credit for state death taxes will be phased out beginning in 2002. The credit allowed under current law will be reduced by 25 percent in 2002, by 50 percent in 2003, and by 75 percent in 2004. In 2005, the credit is repealed and replaced with an estate tax deduction for death tax paid to any state or the District of Columbia.

When Will You Get Your Rebate Check?

The Internal Revenue Service (IRS) began mailing out tax rebate checks the week of July 23, 2001. Over 90 million checks will be mailed by the end of the year to individuals who reported taxable income and tax liability (after nonrefundable credits such as the child tax credit or education credits) on their 2000 tax returns. No rebate checks will be sent to those who could be claimed as someone else's dependent for 2000 or to nonresident aliens.

Assuming you have filed your 2000 tax return, the timing of your check should follow the following schedule, based on the last two digits of your Social Security number. If you filed a joint return for 2000, the first Social Security number on the return determines the mailing date. The last checks to individuals who filed by the April 16 due date should be mailed by the IRS the week of September 24. If you have not received your check by October 5, call the IRS at (800) 829-1040. Taxpayers who have not yet filed for 2000 will have to wait until the IRS processes their 2000 returns for the rebate process to be triggered. The IRS will mail rebate checks until late December 2001.

Social Security Ends With:	*Check Arrival Week:*
00–09	July 23
10–19	July 30
20–29	August 6
30–39	August 13
40–49	August 20
50–59	August 27
60–69	September 3
70–79	September 10
80–89	September 17
90–99	September 24

If you have moved since filing your 2000 return, file a change of address form with the U.S. Postal Service. The IRS updates its address files weekly using the Postal Service's National Change of Address database. You may also notify the IRS directly by filing Form 8822.

The maximum rebate check, based on filing status for 2000, is $300 for single taxpayers and married persons filing separately, $500 for heads of household, and $600 for married couples filing jointly and qualifying widow(er)s. If tax liability for 2000 (after nonrefundable credits) is less than this maximum amount, the rebate will be limited to the smaller of either the liability or 5 percent of the 2000 taxable income. Where less than the maximum $300, $500, or $600 rebate is received, the difference may be available as a tax credit on your 2001 return.

An expected rebate may be reduced or eliminated if you owe the IRS back taxes, have an unpaid Federal student loan, or have past-due child support obligations. If you are paying taxes to the IRS under an installment arrangement, the rebate amount will be applied to the balance of taxes owed, but regular required monthly payments should be continued. If any of these offsets are made, the IRS will provide an explanation.

States Likely to Block Indirect Tax on Rebate

There is a possibility that the rebate checks could slightly raise the state tax owed for taxpayers in the following states that allow a deduction for federal taxes paid: Alabama, Iowa, Louisiana, Missouri, Montana, North Dakota, Oklahoma, Oregon, and Utah. If the deduction for federal tax is reduced, taxable income on the state return would be increased, raising the state tax owed by a small amount. Although some of these states might lose considerable revenue if the rebates are exempted from the deduction offset, it is expected that political pressure will force most of them to shield the rebates from indirect state tax.

Originally published in J.K. Lasser's Monthly Tax Letter, June 2001. Distributed by Prentice Hall Direct of Paramus, New Jersey.

CHAPTER 1

Income Tax Rate Reductions*

Individual Income Tax Structure

Our tax system is a progressive system. This somewhat ironic term stems from the fact that as a taxpayer's income increases, so does the marginal tax rate. Since 1993, marginal rates have been based on a five-bracket rate structure: 15 percent, 28 percent, 31 percent, 36 percent and 39.6 percent. The new law changes this. The centerpiece of the new law is a reduction of tax rates, starting in 2001. A new 10 percent bracket has been created as the lowest bracket. Between 2001 and 2006, gradual reductions will be made to the prior-law rates over 15 percent. By 2006, there will be six brackets: 10 percent, 15 percent, 25 percent, 28 percent, 33 percent, and 35 percent.

*Without an act of Congress, all of the new laws enacted by the 2001 Tax Act will disappear (or "sunset") at the end of 2010, and the rules in effect prior to the 2001 Tax Act will again be law. See the Introduction for more details.

TABLE 1.1 Prior-Law Tax Rates

Filing Status	15 Percent Bracket Ended At:	28 Percent Bracket Ended At:	31 Percent Bracket Ended At:	36 Percent Bracket Ended At:	39.6 Percent Bracket Applied To:
Single	$26,250	$ 63,550	$132,600	$288,350	Over $288,350
Head of household	$35,150	$ 90,800	$147,050	$288,350	Over $288,350
Married filing jointly	$43,850	$105,950	$161,450	$288,350	Over $288,350
Married filing separately	$21,925	$ 52,975	$ 80,725	$144,175	Over $144,175

Pre-2001 Tax Act

Since 1993, taxable income has fallen into five brackets: 15 percent, 28 percent, 31 percent, 36 percent, and 39.6 percent. For the year 2000, these rates applied in the manner outlined in Table 1.1.

New Law

A new 10 percent tax bracket has been created for a portion of the income that was previously taxed at 15 percent. (See Table 1.2.) Rates higher than 15 percent are reduced effective July 1, 2001, in effect giving a half-a-percent reduction for the calendar year 2001. Between 2002 and 2006, these rates will

TABLE 1.2 Income Levels Included in the New 10 Percent Bracket

Filing Status	Taxable Income Subject to 10 Percent Rate
Single	Up to $6,000
Head of household	Up to $10,000
Married filing jointly	Up to $12,000
Married filing separately	Up to $6,000
These income levels will not change until after 2007. Starting in 2008 the 10 percent bracket will include taxable income of:	
Single	Up to $7,000
Head of household	Up to $10,000
Married filing jointly	Up to $14,000
Married filing separately	Up to $7,000
These income levels will be adjusted for inflation starting in 2009.	

continue to decline gradually. (The 10 percent and 15 percent rates will not fall.) In 2006 the phase-down will be complete; the rates at that time will be 10 percent, 15 percent, 25 percent, 28 percent, 33 percent, and 35 percent. (See Table 1.3.)

Most taxpayers will not have to wait until they file to get the benefit of the 10 percent rate for 2001. The savings from the creation of the 10 percent bracket take the form of either a rebate check received from the IRS in the second half of 2001 or a tax credit claimed on the 2001 tax return, as discussed later in the chapter. Congress provided the rebate checks in the hope that taxpayers would spend the money and stimulate the economy.

TIP

To reflect the reduction in tax rates higher than 15 percent, the IRS provided employers with new withholding tables for wages paid after June 30, 2001.

TABLE 1.3 Regular Income Tax Rate Reductions

Calendar Year	28% Rate Reduced To:	31% Rate Reduced To:	36% Rate Reduced To:	39.6% Rate Reduced To:
2001 (effective rate)	27.5%	30.5%	35.5%	39.1%
2002–2003	27%	30%	35%	38.6%
2004–2005	26%	29%	34%	37.6%
2006 and later	25%	28%	33%	35%

Tax Rates for 2001 under the New Law

The tax rate schedules for 2001 are outlined in Table 1.4. The rates reflect the 1 percent reduction to the rates over 15 percent that took effect July 1, 2001, resulting in an overall half-point rate reduction for the year. Note that the new 10 percent bracket is not included in the rate schedules. Although the 10 percent rate applies for 2001, the benefit of the rate is received either through a rebate check from the IRS or a tax credit claimed on your 2001 return. Starting in 2002, the 10 percent bracket will be reflected in the IRS tax tables and rate schedules, and taken into account by employers for wage withholding purposes.

If your taxable income for 2001 is less than $100,000, you will not use the tax rate schedules to figure your tax liability. Instead, you will use IRS tax tables to look up your tax after determining your taxable income. The amount of tax shown in the tax tables will be close to the amount computed under the rate schedules, so you may use the rate schedule shown in Table 1.4 for your filing status to esti-

Schedule X—Use if your filing status is **Single**

If taxable income is:		The tax is—		of the amount over—
Over—	But not over—			
$0	$27,050	- - - - - - - 15%		$0
27,050	65,550	$4,057.50 +	27.5%	27,050
65,550	136,750	14,645.00 +	30.5%	65,550
136,750	297,350	36,361.00 +	35.5%	136,750
297,350	- - - - - - -	93,374.00 +	39.1%	297,350

Schedule Y-1— Use if your filing status is **Married filing jointly or Qualified widow(er)**

If taxable income is:		The tax is—		of the amount over—
Over—	But not over—			
$0	$45,200	- - - - - - - 15%		$0
45,200	109,250	$6,780.00 +	27.5%	45,200
109,250	166,500	24,393.75 +	30.5%	109,250
166,500	297,350	41,855.00 +	35.5%	166,500
297,350	- - - - - - -	88,306.75 +	39.1%	297,350

Schedule Y-2 — Use if your filing status is **Married filing separately**

If taxable income is:		The tax is—		of the amount over—
Over—	But not over—			
$0	$22,600	- - - - - - - 15%		$0
22,600	54,625	$3,390.00 +	27.5%	22,600
54,625	83,250	12,196.88 +	30.5%	54,625
83,250	148,675	20,927.50 +	35.5%	83,250
148,675	- - - - - - -	44,153.38 +	39.1%	148,675

Schedule Z — Use if your filing status is **Head of Household**

If taxable income is:		The tax is—		of the amount over—
Over—	But not over—			
$0	$36,250	- - - - - - - 15%		$0
36,250	93,650	$5,437.50 +	27.5%	36,250
93,650	151,650	21,222.50 +	30.5%	93,650
151,650	297,350	38,912.50 +	35.5%	151,650
297,350	- - - - - - -	90,636.00 +	39.1%	297,350

TABLE 1.4 Tax Rate Schedules for 2001

Example 1

You are single and after deductions you have taxable income for 2001 of $34,000. You will use the tax tables to figure your 2001 income tax liability, but the $5,968.75 tax from the rate schedule in Table 1.4 will closely approximate the tax from the IRS tax table.

Tax on first $27,050	$4,057.50
27.5 percent tax on excess $6,950 ($34,000 – $27,050)	$1,911.25
Total tax	$5,968.75

The reduction in your top rate from 28 percent to 27.5 percent saves you only $34.75 (0.5 percent × $6,950). However, the $300 rebate check or tax credit for 2001, reflecting the new 10 percent bracket, provides an additional tax savings.

Example 2

You are married filing jointly, and after deductions you have taxable income of $103,000 for 2001.

Tax on first $45,200	$ 6,780.00
27.5 percent tax on excess $57,800 ($103,000 – $45,200)	$15,895.00
Total tax	$ 22,675.00

The reduction in the 28 percent rate to 27.5 percent lowers your tax by $289 (0.5 percent × $57,800). A $600 rebate check or tax credit for 2001 provides an additional tax savings.

Tax Planning Opportunity?

Two main tenets of tax planning are income deferral and deduction acceleration. These traditional year-end planning strategies may prove especially advantageous for many taxpayers as tax rate reductions are phased in between now and 2006.

As tax rates decline, deductions will become less valuable. Discretionary itemized deductions such as charitable contribution deductions provide a larger tax savings when taken in the years when rates are higher. However, for certain high-bracket taxpayers who are currently subject to the overall limit on itemized deductions or phaseout of personal exemptions, deductions may prove more valuable after 2005 when these restrictions are gradually eliminated (see later in the chapter).

On the income side, declining tax rates increase the incentive to defer income to later years. Income deferral is not a practical option for many taxpayers, but where possible, deferring income such as a bonus or self-employment fee to a later year could lower the tax on the income.

mate your regular income tax liability for 2001. Your effective liability will be reduced by the rebate check you received or tax credit to which you are entitled, based on the 10 percent rate.

Congress has provided an estimate of what the tax brackets will be in 2006 when the tax rate reductions are fully phased in. Table 1.5 is only a projection, since the exact amounts of income subject to each rate depend on inflation adjustments.

TABLE 1.5 Projected Income Tax Brackets for 2006

If Taxable Income Is:	But Not Over:	Then Regular Income Tax Equals:
Single Individuals		
$0	$6,000	10 percent of taxable income
$6,000	$30,950	$600, plus 15 percent of the amount over $6,000
$30,950	$74,950	$4,342.50, plus 25 percent of the amount over $30,950
$74,950	$156,300	$15,342.50, plus 28 percent of the amount over $74,950
$156,300	$339,850	$38,120.50, plus 33 percent of the amount over $156,300
Over $339,850		$98,692, plus 35 percent of the amount over $339,850
Heads of Households:		
$0	$10,000	10 percent of taxable income
$10,000	$41,450	$1,000, plus 15 percent of the amount over $10,000
$41,450	$107,000	$5,717.50, plus 25 percent of the amount over $41,450
$107,000	$173,300	$22,105, plus 28 percent of the amount over $107,000
$173,300	$339,850	$40,669, plus 33 percent of the amount over $173,300
Over $339,850		$95,630.50, plus 35 percent of the amount over $339,850
Married Individuals Filing Joint Returns		
$0	$12,000	10 percent of taxable income
$12,000	*$57,850	$1,200, plus 15 percent of the amount over $12,000
$57,850	$124,900	$8,077.50, plus 25 percent of the amount over $57,850
$124,900	$190,300	$24,840, plus 28 percent of the amount over $124,900
$190,300	$339,850	$43,152, plus 33 percent of the amount over $190,300
Over $339,850		$92,503.50, plus 35 percent of the amount over $339,850

*The end point of the 15 percent rate bracket for married individuals filing joint returns also reflects the phase-in of the increase in the size of the 15 percent bracket, discussed in Chapter 2, "Tax Relief for Families."

Rebate Checks

By now, the IRS should have notified you about how large a tax rebate check to expect, or you may have even received your check. The rebate checks, representing the tax savings attributable to the new 10 percent tax rate bracket, are an advance refund of a 5 percent tax credit for 2001. To get the tax cut in the hands of taxpayers as soon as possible and provide a stimulus to the economy, Congress decided to authorize rebate checks to most taxpayers based on their 2000 filing information. The rebate is 5 percent (the difference between the 15 percent and 10 percent rates) of the amount of taxable income eligible for the new 10 percent rate. Thus, the maximum rebate is $300 for single taxpayers and married persons filing separately (5 percent of first $6,000 of taxable income), $500 for heads of household (5 percent of first $10,000 of taxable income), and $600 for married couples filing jointly and qualified widows (5 percent of first $12,000 of taxable income).

Generally, all taxpayers with federal income tax liability for 2000 will get a rebate check, unless they could be claimed as another taxpayer's dependent. If a taxpayer's 2000 tax liability after nonrefundable credits was less than the maximum rebate ($300, $500, or $600), the rebate is limited to the smaller of the liability or 5 percent of taxable income for 2000. The IRS began mailing out rebate checks at the end of July. Most of the checks will be delivered by October, although taxpayers who filed their 2000 returns late will not receive their rebates until the latter part of 2001. No checks will be issued after December 31, 2001.

Taxpayers who did not have income tax liability for 2000 will not receive a rebate check, but if they owe tax for 2001, the 5 percent credit may be claimed on their 2001 return, so long as they are not another taxpayer's dependent. The new law does not allow students or others claimed as dependents to obtain any benefit from the 10 percent rate for 2001; they are not entitled to the rebate or to the credit. Nonresident aliens are also ineligible.

When eligible taxpayers file their 2001 tax returns, they will complete a worksheet included in the IRS tax instructions to determine the amount of the credit they are entitled to for 2001. The maximum credit, based on 2001 taxable income, is $300, $500, or $600, the same as the maximum rebate check. Since the rebate is an advance payment of the credit, the credit figured on the IRS worksheet will be reduced by the amount of the rebate check received, if any. For many taxpayers, the allowable credit will be completely eliminated by the rebate check. If the credit is more than the rebate check, which could happen where little or no tax was paid for 2000 but a larger amount of tax is due for 2001, the excess is allowed as a credit against the tax owed on the 2001 return. If the rebate check is more than the allowable credit based on 2001 taxable income and liability, the difference does not have to be repaid to the IRS.

> **TIP**
>
> No reductions were made in the alternative minimum tax (AMT) rates, although alternative minimum tax exemption amounts were increased (see discussion later in the chapter). Projected tax savings of many individuals may be significantly diminished after the application of the alternative minimum tax.

Repeal of Phaseout of Itemized Deductions

As a person's income increases, the tax rate increases in many ways—beyond the simple tax bracket. Many tax benefits (such as the itemized deduction) that most of us take for granted are disallowed or significantly reduced due to a higher income level. This results in what is essentially another tax on income. The new tax law removes some of these extra taxes.

Pre-2001 Tax Act

Taxpayers with an adjusted gross income in excess of $132,950 ($66,475 for married couples filing separate returns) in 2001 will begin to find their itemized deductions reduced. The total amount of their otherwise allowable itemized deductions (this doesn't include medical expenses, investment interest, and casualty, theft, or wagering losses) is reduced by 3 percent of the amount their adjusted gross income exceeds $132,950 (or $66,475). (These amounts are adjusted annually for inflation.) This reduction is limited—otherwise allowable itemized deductions may not be reduced by more than 80 percent.

Example

Ann and Bob have an adjusted gross income of $240,000 and itemized deductions of $12,000 in 2001. As mentioned, the adjusted gross income threshold for this year is $132,950. Under these circumstances, their itemized deductions would be reduced by $3,212 (3 percent × [$240,000 − $132,950]) for a total of only $8,788.

TIP

A deferral of deductions may be warranted if, for example, in the year 2005 a taxpayer would be subject to the limitation on deductions.

TIP

The repeal of the itemized deduction limitation is good news for high-earner taxpayers, although the 2010 effective date for full relief is many years away and only a year before all the provisions of the Act are scheduled to sunset under Congressional budget rules.

New Law

The limitation on itemized deductions is repealed for tax years beginning after 2009. The repeal is to be phased in over five years beginning after 2005 (so, for the next few years, don't get too excited). The limitation is reduced by one-third in tax years beginning in 2006 and 2007, and by two-thirds in tax years beginning in 2008 and 2009. This

Example 1

In 2006, Ann and Bob have an adjusted gross income of $240,000 and itemized deductions of $12,000. If we assume that the adjusted gross income threshold for 2006 is $160,000 (remember, it is adjusted for inflation), then the reduction in otherwise allowable deductions would be $2,400 (3 percent × [$240,000 – $160,000]). Up to this point, the calculation is the same as it was earlier. But, as it is 2006, the limitation is to be reduced by one-third. So, Ann and Bob's new limitation reduction is equal to $2,400 reduced by one-third or $800, so the actual reduction is $1,600. Thus, their allowable itemized deduction is $12,000 – $1,600 or $10,400.

Example 2

In 2008, Ann and Bob have an adjusted gross income of $250,000 and itemized deductions of $15,000. If we assume that the adjusted gross income threshold for 2008 is $170,000, then the reduction in otherwise allowable deductions would be $2,400 (3 percent × [$250,000 – $170,000]). The $2,400 is then reduced by two-thirds or $1,600, so that the limitation reduction is $800. Thus, their allowable itemized deduction is $15,000 – $800 or $14,200.

Example 3

In 2010, Ann and Bob have an adjusted gross income of $260,000 and itemized deductions of $17,500. At this point, the limitation will have been completely repealed and their itemized deductions will not be subject to any limitation.

system effectively keeps the tax code complex. Let's look at some examples.

Repeal of Phaseout of Personal Exemptions

Much like the phaseout of itemized deductions outlined in the preceding section, a phaseout of personal exemptions also increases the higher-income taxpayer's taxes. The new law sets in place a plan to eventually eliminate this system.

Pre-2001 Tax Act

The deduction for personal exemptions is phased out ratably for taxpayers with adjusted gross incomes over certain thresholds. The thresholds are adjusted annually for inflation. For 2001 they are:

Single individual	$132,950
Married filing jointly	$199,450
Head of household	$166,200
Married filing separately	$99,725

New Law

Much like the repeal of the itemized deduction limitation outlined earlier, the repeal for personal exemptions is phased in over five years beginning in 2006. The phaseout is completely repealed for tax years beginning after 2009. Under this system, the personal exemptions phaseout that would normally apply is reduced by one-third in tax years beginning in 2006 and 2007. For tax years beginning in 2008 and 2009, it is reduced by two-thirds.

TIP

This is good news for high-income families with many dependents, although the 2010 effective date for full relief is many years away and only a year before all the provisions of the Act are scheduled to sunset under Congressional budget rules.

Example 1

In 2006, the personal exemptions claimed by Carol and Dave would be reduced by $3,000 under pre-Act law. As it is 2006, the new tax law calls for this phaseout to be reduced by one-third. Thus, their personal exemptions phaseout is reduced by $1,000, meaning their personal exemptions would be reduced by only $2,000.

Example 2

In 2008 the personal exemptions claimed by Carol and Dave would be reduced by $3,000 under pre-Act law. As it is now 2008, the new tax law calls for this phaseout to be reduced by two-thirds. Thus, their personal exemptions phaseout is reduced by $2,000. In turn, their personal exemptions would be reduced by only $1,000.

Example 3

In 2010 the personal exemptions claimed by Carol and Dave would not be subject to any reduction, regardless of income level.

Alternative Minimum Tax Relief

Critics of the 2001 Tax Act warn that many of the income tax reductions promised will not be realized by millions of taxpayers who are expected to become subject to the alternative minimum tax (AMT). This concern was not adequately addressed in the Act. The new law provides a minor increase in the AMT exemption.

Pre-2001 Tax Act

An alternative minimum tax (AMT) is imposed on individuals to the extent that the tentative minimum tax exceeds the regular tax. An individual's tentative minimum tax generally is an amount equal to the sum of (1) 26 percent of the first $175,000 ($87,500 in the case of a married individual filing a separate return) of alternative minimum taxable income (AMTI) in excess of an exemption amount and (2) 28 percent of the remaining AMTI. AMTI is the individual's taxable income adjusted to take account of specified preferences and adjustments.

The AMT exemption amounts are: (1) $45,000 in the case of married individuals filing a joint return and surviving spouses; (2) $33,750 in the case of other unmarried individuals; and (3) $22,500 in the case of married individuals filing a separate return, estates, and trusts. The exemption amounts are phased out by an amount equal to 25 percent of the amount by which the individual's AMTI exceeds (1) $150,000 in the case of married individuals filing a joint return and surviving spouses, (2) $112,500 in the case of other unmarried individuals, and (3) $75,000 in the case of married individuals filing separate returns or an estate or a trust. The exemption amounts, the threshold phase-out amounts, and rate brackets are not indexed for inflation.

New Law

The AMT exemption amount is increased for married couples filing joint returns and surviving spouses by $4,000. The AMT exemption amounts for other individuals (i.e., unmarried individuals and married individuals filing separate returns) are increased by $2,000. The provision applies to tax years beginning after 2000, and beginning before 2005.

This temporary provision is intended to reduce the number of taxpayers subject to the alternative minimum tax. However, it is unlikely to offset the number of taxpayers that will be subject to the alternative minimum tax due to the decrease in marginal tax rates without a corresponding reduction of the alternative minimum tax.

CHAPTER 2

Tax Relief for Families*

Tax Benefits Relating to Children

Increase and Expansion of Child Tax Credit

In an effort to make the tax code more family friendly, the Taxpayer Relief Act of 1997 added the child tax credit. This credit is designed to offset the expense of raising children. It is based solely on the number of dependent children in a taxpayer's family.

*Without an act of Congress, all of the new laws enacted by the 2001 Tax Act will disappear (or "sunset") at the end of 2010, and the rules in effect prior to the 2001 Tax Act will again be law. See the Introduction for more details.

Pre-2001 Tax Act

An individual may claim a $500 tax credit for each qualifying child under the age of 17. The credit is phased out for individuals with income over certain thresholds. Specifically, the credit is reduced by $50 for each $1,000 (or fraction thereof) of modified adjusted gross income (MAGI) over the following thresholds:

> **TIP**
>
> A qualifying child is a dependent that is your child, stepchild, grandchild, great grandchild, or adopted child.

Single	$75,000
Head of household	$ 75,000
Married filing jointly	$110,000
Married filing separately	$ 55,000

The credit is generally not refundable. However, for families with three or more qualifying children, you may be entitled to a refundable credit called the "additional child credit." To claim this additional credit, file Form 8812.

> **TIP**
>
> To figure the credit reduction, use the worksheet that comes with the Form 1040 instruction booklet.

New Law

For 2001, the child tax credit is increased to $600, phased in to $1,000 by 2010. (See Table 2.1.) The credit phaseout based on income has not been changed.

The child credit is allowed to the extent of the full amount of the taxpayer's regular income tax and alternative minimum tax. This is a permanent extension of the rule in effect for 2000 and 2001.

The new tax law makes the credit partially refundable regardless of the number of children you have. That means that you can claim the credit even if you don't owe any taxes. There is a limitation on this. The credit is refundable to the extent of 10 percent of the taxpayer's earned income in excess of $10,000 for calendar years 2001 to 2004. What does this mean? Let's look at an example:

Example

Anne and Bob have three children and earned income of $15,000 in 2002. Their child tax credit totals $1,800 for the year ($600 per child). But their earned income exceeds $10,000 by $5,000. The limitation just outlined prescribes that the family will be able to get a refund of only $500 (10 percent × [$15,000 − $10,000]). Thus, their refundable credit is effectively reduced by $1,300.

The limitation percentage is increased to 15 percent for calendar years 2005 and thereafter. The $10,000 amount is indexed for inflation beginning in 2002.

TABLE 2.1 Increase of the Child Tax Credit

CALENDAR YEAR	CREDIT AMOUNT PER CHILD
2001–2004	$ 600
2005–2008	$ 700
2009	$ 800
2010 and later	$1,000

The rule for families of three or more children, as outlined earlier in the pre-Act section, remains essentially unchanged. In this situation, families with three or more children are allowed a refundable credit for the amount by which the taxpayer's Social Security taxes exceed the taxpayer's earned income credit (as under prior law), if that amount is greater than the refundable credit based on the taxpayer's earned income in excess of $10,000.

> **TIP**
>
> The refundable portion of the credit does not constitute income and will not be treated as a resource for purposes of determining eligibility or the amount or nature of benefits or assistance under any federal program or any state or local program financed with federal funds.

Extension and Expansion of Adoption Tax Benefits

Beginning in 1997, taxpayers have been allowed two tax breaks for adopting children. The first is a tax credit that helps taxpayers offset their adoption expenses. The second is an income exclusion for employer-paid or -reimbursed adoption expenses. The 2001 tax law furthers these benefits by expanding both the credit and the exclusion.

Pre-2001 Tax Act

CREDIT. A tax credit is allowed for qualified adoption expenses. The maximum credit is $5,000 per child ($6,000 for a special needs child). The credit is phased out for taxpayers with high incomes. Specifically, it begins to phase out ratably for taxpayers with modified adjusted gross incomes of $75,000 and is completely eliminated for those earning $115,000 or more.

The credit generally reduces regular income tax and alternative minimum tax. But, for years after 2001, the credit is allowed only to the extent that the individual's regular income tax liability exceeds the individual's tentative minimum tax.

The adoption credit for special needs children is permanent; the adoption credit with respect to other children expires on December 31, 2001.

Example

Don and Elizabeth adopt a child in 2002. Their expenses total $4,500. For the year, their income tax liability is $4,000 while their tentative minimum tax is $3,000. If the old law applied, they would be limited to a credit of only $1,000 ($4,000 − $3,000).

EXCLUSION. Taxpayers are allowed to exclude from income money that their employer provides to aid in the adoption process. The maximum amount excludable is $5,000 and is allowed for qualified adoption expenses paid or reimbursed by an employer under an adoption assistance program. The maximum excludable amount is $6,000 for special needs adoptions. The exclusion is phased out ratably for taxpayers with modified adjusted gross incomes between $75,000 and $115,000. The exclusion expires on December 31, 2001.

As might be expected, adoption expenses paid or reimbursed under an adoption assistance program are not eligible for the credit. Taxpayers should note that they may be eligible for the credit and also the exclusion if they are used for separate expenses.

The exclusion is scheduled to expire on December 31, 2001.

Example

Don and Elizabeth adopt a child. They receive $1,000 from their employer's adoption assistance program. Their total expenses are $3,000, $2,000 of which they cover on their own. Thus, they will be able to exclude the $1,000 from income while also claiming the $2,000 credit.

New Law

CREDIT. For years after 2001, the maximum credit has been increased to $10,000 per child, including special needs children. For special needs adoptions after 2002, the $10,000 credit is provided for the year the adoption is finalized, regardless of whether the taxpayer has qualified adoption expenses. After 2002, the credit for special needs adoptions is no longer tied to the amount of expenditures incurred by the taxpayer. However, starting in 2002, no credit is allowed unless the adoption is finalized.

Example

Don and Elizabeth adopt a special needs child. The adoption is finalized in 2003. Their total expenses for the adoption amounted to $3,500. Since they adopted a special needs child, the new tax law will allow them to take a credit of $10,000 in 2003.

After 2001, the income phaseout range is increased to begin at $150,000 of modified adjusted gross income and be completely eliminated for taxpayers with a modified adjusted gross incomes of $190,000 or more.

The credit is permanently extended beyond 2001 for adoption of non–special needs children. For all years after 2001, the credit is allowed against the alternative minimum tax as well as regular income tax.

EXCLUSION. The exclusion has been permanently extended and increased to $10,000 per eligible child, including special needs children. For special needs adoptions after 2002, the $10,000 exclusion applies, regardless of whether the taxpayer had qualified adoption expenses.

After 2001, the income

TIP

Like the credit, the exclusion for special needs adoptions is not tied to actual expenditures after 2002.

phaseout range is increased to begin at $150,000 of modified adjusted gross income and be completely eliminated for taxpayers with modified adjusted gross incomes of $190,000 or more.

The credit and exclusion dollar limitations and phaseout ranges will be adjusted for inflation after 2002.

Expansion of Dependent Care Tax Credit

The dependent care credit is designed to offset a taxpayer's expense of hiring someone to care for children or other dependents so that the taxpayer can work.

Pre-2001 Tax Act

CREDIT. A taxpayer who maintains a household that includes one or more qualifying individuals may claim a nonrefundable credit against the taxpayer's income tax liability. The maximum available credit is 30 percent of employment-related expenses. Eligible employment-related expenses are limited to $2,400 if there is one qualifying individual or $4,800 if there are two or more qualifying individuals.

The 30 percent credit rate is reduced, but not below 20 percent, by 1 percentage point for each $2,000 (or fraction thereof) of adjusted gross income above $10,000. The credit is not available to married taxpayers unless they file a joint return.

Thus, the maximum credit is $720 if there is one qualifying

TIP

Before 2003, the credit percentage is reduced to 20 percent for taxpayers with adjusted gross incomes over $28,000.

individual and $1,440 if there are two or more qualifying individuals. The applicable dollar limit ($2,400/$4,800) of otherwise eligible employment-related expenses is reduced by any amount excluded from income under an employer-provided dependent care assistance program.

TIP

Dependent care expenses excluded from income are not eligible for the dependent care tax credit (see Example 1).

Example 1

Eddie has one child under the age of 13 for whom he is eligible to claim a dependency exemption. He has an adjusted gross income (AGI) of $10,000. Eddie incurs $3,000 in child care expenses for the child in order to work at ABC corporation. Eddie receives $1,000 of dependent care assistance provided by ABC, which he excludes from income. The dollar limit of eligible employment-related expenses for the dependent care credit must be reduced by the exclusion. Thus, Eddie's eligible dependent care expenses are limited to $1,400 ($2,400 – $1,000). Since his AGI does not exceed $10,000, he is allowed the full 30 percent credit; on his tax return, Eddie may claim a credit of $420 (30 percent × $1,400).

Example 2

Eddie has adjusted gross income of $20,000. His credit rate is reduced by 5 percent (1 percent for each $2,000 increment above $10,000) to 25 percent. If Eddie's adjusted gross income was over $28,000, his credit rate would be the minimum rate of 20 percent.

EXCLUSION. Amounts paid or incurred by an employer for dependent care assistance provided to an employee generally are excluded from the employee's gross income and wages if the assistance is furnished under a program meeting certain federal requirements. The requirements include that the program be described in writing, satisfy certain nondiscrimination rules, and provide for notification to all eligible employees. Dependent care assistance expenses eligible for the exclusion are defined the same as employment-related expenses with respect to a qualifying individual under the dependent care tax credit.

The dependent care exclusion is limited to $5,000 per year—except for a married taxpayer filing a separate return, who is limited to only $2,500.

New Law

CREDIT. Starting in 2003, the maximum amount of eligible employment-related expenses will increase from $2,400 to $3,000 if there is one qualifying individual and from $4,800 to $6,000 if there are two or more qualifying individuals. The maximum credit is increased to 35 percent for 2003 and later years. The 35 percent credit is reduced, but not below 20 percent, by 1 percentage point for each $2,000 (or fraction thereof) of adjusted gross income above $15,000.

TIP

After 2002, a 20 percent dependent care credit will be allowed for taxpayers with adjusted gross income over $43,000.

> ## Example
>
> In 2003, Eddie has adjusted gross income of $21,000. His credit rate would be 32 percent (35 percent reduced by 3 percent [1 percentage point for each $2,000 salary increment or portion thereof above $15,000]). If Eddie's adjusted gross income increased to any amount over $43,000, his credit rate would be 20 percent.

EXCLUSION. The new law does not change the exclusion rules for employer-provided dependent care assistance.

Marriage Penalty Relief

A married couple generally is treated as one tax unit that must pay tax on the couple's total taxable income. Although married couples may elect to file separate returns, the rate sched-

> Much has been written about the "marriage penalty" as Congress has grappled with the issue of providing relief for perceived inequities based on marital status. A marriage penalty exists when the combined tax liability of a married couple filing a joint return exceeds the total tax they would have to pay if they were single. On the other hand, a "marriage bonus" exists when the combined tax liability of a married couple on a joint return is less than the total tax that would be due if they were single. Typically, a marriage bonus occurs when only one spouse has income or when there is great disparity between the incomes of the spouses, while a marriage penalty results when the spouses' incomes are roughly equivalent.

ules and other provisions are structured so that filing separate returns usually results in a higher tax than filing a joint return.

The new law provides partial marriage penalty relief for joint filers in the form of a higher standard deduction and a wider 15 percent bracket, but the changes are delayed until 2005 and then phased in over several years.

Standard Deduction Marriage Penalty Relief

Pre-2001 Tax Act

Taxpayers who do not itemize deductions may choose the basic standard deduction, which is subtracted from adjusted gross income (AGI) in arriving at taxable income. The size of the basic standard deduction varies according to filing status and is adjusted annually for inflation. For 2001, the basic standard deduction amount for single filers is 60 percent of the basic standard deduction amount for married couples filing joint returns.

TIP

Two unmarried individuals have standard deductions that when added together exceed the standard deduction for a married couple filing a joint return.

New Law

From 2005 to 2009, the basic standard deduction for a married couple filing a joint return will be increased until it is

> The basic standard deduction for unmarried individuals filing a single return and for married couples filing separately will be the same starting in 2005. The phased-in increases to the standard deduction apply to all married couples filing jointly, thereby providing a windfall for those enjoying a "marriage bonus," described earlier in the chapter.

twice the basic standard deduction for an unmarried individual filing a single return.

Table 2.2 shows the standard deduction for married couples filing a joint return as a percentage of the standard deduction for single individuals during the phase-in period.

> The increase in the standard deduction available for joint filers is good news for many married couples, but will benefit only those taxpayers who do not itemize deductions. Also, the 2009 effective date for full relief is years away and only two years before all the provisions of the Act are scheduled to sunset under Congressional budget rules.

Expansion of the 15 Percent Rate Bracket for Married Couples Filing Joint Returns

The income tax rate schedules are divided into several ranges of income, known as income brackets. A taxpayer's marginal tax rate increases as his or her income increases. Separate rate schedules apply based on filing status: single individuals (other than heads of household and surviving

TABLE 2.2 Phase-In of Increase of Standard Deduction for Married Couples Filing Joint Returns

CALENDAR YEAR	STANDARD DEDUCTION FOR JOINT RETURNS AS PERCENTAGE OF STANDARD DEDUCTION FOR SINGLE RETURNS
2005	174 percent
2006	184 percent
2007	187 percent
2008	190 percent
2009 and later	200 percent

spouses), heads of household, married individuals filing joint returns (including surviving spouses), and married individuals filing separate returns.

Pre-2001 Tax Act

In general, the bracket break points for single individuals are approximately 60 percent of the rate bracket break points for married couples filing joint returns. For example, the 15 percent income bracket for 2001 ends at taxable income of $27,050 for single filers and $45,200 for married couples filing jointly. (The rate bracket break points for married individuals filing separate returns are exactly one-half of the rate brackets for married individuals filing joint returns.)

New Law

After 2004, the size of the 15 percent regular income tax rate bracket for a married couple filing a joint return will gradually be increased to twice the size of the corresponding rate bracket for a single individual. The increase is phased in over four years, beginning in 2005. Therefore the provision is fully effective for tax years beginning in 2008. Table 2.3 shows the increase in the size of the 15 percent rate bracket during the phase-in period.

Marriage Penalty Relief and Simplification Relating to the Earned Income Credit

Eligible low-income workers are able to claim a refundable earned income credit. The amount of the credit depends on the taxpayer's income and whether the taxpayer has one child, more than one child, or no qualifying children.

TABLE 2.3 Increase in Size of 15 Percent Rate Bracket for Married Couples Filing a Joint Return

TAXABLE YEAR	END POINT OF 15 PERCENT RATE BRACKET FOR MARRIED COUPLE FILING JOINTLY*
2005	180 percent
2006	187 percent
2007	193 percent
2008 and thereafter	200 percent

*Calculated as percentage of end point of 15 percent rate bracket for unmarried individuals.

The earned income credit is not available to married individuals who file separate returns. No earned income credit is allowed if the taxpayer has disqualified income in excess of $2,450 (for 2001) for the tax year. Disqualified income includes interest (taxable and tax-exempt), dividends, net rent and royalty income, net capital gain income, and net passive income that is not self-employment income. In addition, no earned income credit is allowed if an eligible individual is the qualifying child of another taxpayer.

Pre-2001 Tax Act

QUALIFYING CHILD. A qualifying child must meet a relationship test, an age test, and a residence test. First, the qualifying child must be the taxpayer's child, stepchild, adopted child, grandchild, or foster child. Second, the child must be under age 19 (or under age 24 if a full-time student) or permanently disabled regardless of age. Third, the child must live with the taxpayer in the United States for more than half the year (a full year for foster children).

An individual satisfies the relationship test if the individual is the taxpayer's: (1) son or daughter or descendant of either, (2) stepson or stepdaughter; or (3) eligible foster child. An eligible foster child is an individual (1) who is a brother, sister, stepbrother, or stepsister of the taxpayer (or a descendant of any such relative) or who is placed with the taxpayer by an authorized placement agency, and (2) who is cared for by the taxpayer as her or his own child. A married child of the taxpayer is not treated as meeting the relationship test unless the taxpayer can claim that child as a dependent or could have if the taxpayer had not waived the exemption to the noncustodial parent.

TIEBREAKER RULES. If a child qualifies with respect to more than one person, the child is treated as a qualifying child only of the person with the highest modified adjusted gross income.

DEFINITION OF EARNED INCOME. To claim the earned income credit, the taxpayer must have earned income. Earned income consists of wages, salaries, other employee compensation, and net earnings from self-employment. Employee compensation includes anything of value received by the taxpayer from the employer in return for services of the employee, including nontaxable earned income. Nontaxable forms of compensation treated as earned income include the following: (1) elective deferrals under a cash or deferred arrangement or 403(b) annuity; (2) employer contributions for nontaxable fringe benefits, including contributions for accident and health insurance, dependent care, adoption assistance, educational assistance, and miscellaneous fringe benefits; (3) salary reduction contributions under a cafeteria plan; (4) meals and lodging provided for the convenience of the employer, and (5) housing allowance or rental value of a parsonage for the clergy.

CALCULATION OF CREDIT. The maximum earned income credit is phased in as an individual's earned income increases. The credit phases out for individuals with earned income (or if greater, modified adjusted gross income) over certain levels. In the case of a married individual who files a joint return, the earned income credit both for the phase-in and phaseout is calculated based on the couple's combined income.

The credit is determined by multiplying the credit rate by the taxpayer's earned income up to a specified earned income amount. The maximum amount of the credit is the product of the credit rate and the earned income amount. The maximum credit amount applies to taxpayers with (1) earnings at or above the earned income amount and (2) modified adjusted gross income (or earnings, if greater) at or below the phaseout threshold level.

For taxpayers with modified adjusted gross income (or earned income, if greater) in excess of the phaseout threshold, the credit amount is reduced by the phaseout rate multiplied by the amount of earned income (or modified adjusted gross income, if greater) in excess of the phaseout threshold.

TIP

In other words, the credit amount is reduced, falling to zero at the "breakeven" income level—the point where a specified percentage of excess income above the phaseout threshold offsets exactly the maximum amount of the credit.

MARRIAGE PENALTY. The required aggregation of incomes on a joint return and the phaseout formula penalizes some individuals when they marry. They may be allowed a smaller earned income credit than if they were not married and claimed separate credits.

The earned income amount

TIP

For 2001 and earlier years, an individual's alternative minimum tax liability reduces the amount of the refundable earned income credit.

TABLE 2.4 Earned Income Credit Parameters (2001)

	TWO OR MORE QUALIFYING CHILDREN	ONE QUALIFYING CHILD	NO QUALIFYING CHILDREN
Credit rate (percent)	40.00%	34.00%	7.65%
Earned income amount	$10,020	$7,140	$4,760
Maximum credit	$4,008	$2,428	$364
Phaseout begins	$13,090	$13,090	$5,950
Phaseout rate (percent)	21.06%	15.98%	7.65%
Phaseout ends	$32,121	$28,281	$10,710

and the phaseout threshold are adjusted annually for inflation. Table 2.4 shows the earned income credit parameters for 2001.

New Law

PHASEOUT RANGE. For married taxpayers who file a joint return, the beginning and ending of the earned income credit phaseout range is increased starting in 2002. The increase in the phaseout range is outlined in Table 2.5.

The $3,000 amount will be adjusted annually for inflation after 2008.

Beginning in 2002, the phaseout computation will be based on the taxpayer's adjusted gross income, rather than modified adjusted gross income.

QUALIFYING CHILD. After 2001, the relationship test for qualifying children is expanded to include descendants of stepsons or

TABLE 2.5 Increase in the Phaseout Range

TAX YEARS	PHASEOUT RANGE INCREASE
2002, 2003, 2004	$1,000
2005, 2006, 2007	$2,000
2008	$3,000

stepdaughters. As under prior law, an adopted child is treated as a child of the taxpayer by blood. The relationship test is met if the individual is the taxpayer's son, daughter, stepson, stepdaughter, or a descendant of any such individuals. The taxpayer's brother, sister, stepbrother, or stepsister, or a descendant of such an individual, also qualifies if the taxpayer cares for such individual as his or her own child. A foster child satisfies the relationship test as well. A foster child is defined as an individual who is placed with the taxpayer by an authorized placement agency and who is cared for by the taxpayer as his or her own child. In order to be a qualifying child, in all cases the child must have the same principal place of abode as the taxpayer for over one-half of the taxable year.

TIP

The new law eliminates the full-year residency requirement for foster children. Also eliminated is the classification of brothers and sisters and their descendants as foster children.

TIEBREAKER RULES. Beginning in 2002, if an individual would be a qualifying child with respect to more than one taxpayer, and more than one taxpayer claims the earned income credit with respect to that child, then the following tie-breaking rules apply. First, if one of the individuals

The IRS is authorized, beginning in 2004, to use math error authority to deny the earned income credit if the Federal Case Registry of Child Support Orders indicates that the taxpayer is the noncustodial parent of the child with respect to whom the credit is claimed.

claiming the child is the child's parent (or parents who file a joint return), the child is considered the qualifying child of the parent (or parents). Second, if both parents claim the child and the parents do not file a joint return together, then the child is considered a qualifying child of the parent with whom the child resided for the longer period of time during the year, or of the parent with the higher adjusted gross income if the child resided with each of them for the same amount of time. Finally, if none of the taxpayers claiming the child as a qualifying child is the child's parent, the child is considered a qualifying child with respect to the taxpayer with the highest adjusted gross income.

DEFINITION OF EARNED INCOME. The new tax law has altered the definition of earned income to exclude nontaxable employee compensation, beginning in 2002. The exclusion of nontaxable employee compensation from the definition of earned income is designed to simplify the earned income rules. Nontaxable employee compensation was difficult to ascertain, since most nontaxable employee benefits are not reported for tax purposes by the employer.

ALTERNATIVE MINIMUM TAX. The provision that reduces the earned income credit by the amount of an individual's alternative minimum tax is repealed for years after 2001.

Sale of Principal Residence— In Conjunction with Estate Tax Changes

The income tax exclusion for the sale of a principal residence is extended to sales by estates, heirs, and qualified revocable trusts for years after 2009. If the decedent's estate, heir, or qualified trust sells the decedent's principal residence, $250,000 of gain can be excluded on the sale of the residence, provided the decedent owned and used the property as a principal residence for two or more years during the five-year period prior to the sale. In addition, if an heir occupies the property as a principal residence, the decedent's period of ownership and occupancy of the property as a principal residence can be added to the heir's subsequent ownership and occupancy in determining whether the property was owned and occupied for two years as a principal residence. For a more in-depth discussion, see Chapter 4, "Estate, Gift, and Generation-Skipping Transfer Tax Relief."

CHAPTER 3

Tax Relief for Educational Expenses*

The new tax law has provided many new ways to increase your savings for educational expenses. Many of the savings plans (such as the Education IRA and Section 529 qualified tuition plans) have been bolstered to allow taxpayers to increase their contributions or avoid taxes upon withdrawals. All taxpayers looking toward financing an education should be interested in this section.

*Without an act of Congress, all of the new laws enacted by the 2001 Tax Act will disappear (or "sunset") at the end of 2010, and the rules in effect prior to the 2001 Tax Act will again be law. See the Introduction for more details.

Education IRAs

Although IRA stands for individual retirement account, the Education IRA, created by a 1997 tax law, is not used for retirement at all. It is, rather, a vehicle designed to help individuals save for their children's college educations. Contributions to the Education IRA must be made on behalf of children under 18 years of age, and the distributions must be used for qualified educational expenses.

Contributions to Education IRAs are not tax deductible, but the investment income the IRA earns will not be taxed as long as the money stays within the plan. The real benefit of the Education IRA is that distributions used for qualified education costs are not subject to taxation. This means that your gains will be forever sheltered from taxation.

Pre-2001 Tax Act

CONTRIBUTIONS. Through the year 2001, contributions to Education IRAs are limited to $500 per designated child per year. The $500 annual limit per child applies regardless of how many individuals make contributions on behalf of the child, or how many Education IRAs are set up for the child. Any contributions made over the $500 limit are subject to a 6 percent excise tax each year until the excess is removed. The low $500 contribution limit has been criticized as inadequate, creating little incentive to set up Education IRAs.

INCOME LIMITATIONS. The $500 contribution limit is available to single taxpayers with a modified adjusted gross income (MAGI) of up to $95,000 or MAGI up to $150,000 if filing a joint return. The contribution limit is reduced on a pro rata basis for MAGIs between $95,000 and $110,000 or between $150,000 and $160,000 for joint filers.

TAX TREATMENT OF DISTRIBUTIONS. Under pre-2001 Tax Act law, withdrawals from Education IRAs are tax-free if used for higher education (after high school) expenses such as tuition, fees, books, supplies, equipment, and limited room and board. In a move that seems to be designed to encourage students to live on campus, the allowable qualified expense for room and board is limited to $2,500 in the case of students living off campus. If withdrawals exceed qualified higher expenses, a portion allocable to earnings is taxable and the taxable portion is subject to a 10 percent penalty unless a penalty exception applies.

If a child's Education IRA balance is not used for college, it may be rolled over tax free to an Education IRA of a sibling or other family member who is under age 30.

New Law

CONTRIBUTIONS. For 2002 and beyond, the annual per-student contribution limit has been increased to $2,000 per year. The 6 percent tax on excess contributions applies for amounts over $2,000. The in-

TIP

The deadline for removing excess contributions has been extended to May 30 of the following tax year.

> **TIP**
>
> Contributing to an Education IRA won't reduce the amount you can contribute to your own traditional IRA or Roth IRA.

creased contribution limit makes an Education IRA much more attractive.

Contributions for 2002 and later can be made up until the original return due date for the year of the contributions—the same rule as for traditional and Roth IRAs. This means that you can contribute to an Education IRA for 2002 until April 15, 2003.

INCOME LIMITATIONS. The new law raises the income limits for married couples filing jointly. Starting in 2002, the maximum $2,000 Education IRA contribution can be made by a couple with an MAGI up to $190,000, with the limit phasing out between $190,000 and $220,000. This is double the phaseout range for single filers.

> **TIP**
>
> There are ways to get around the income limits on Education IRA contributors. Remember that anyone, including the child, can contribute. So the $2,000 maximum can be divided among each of four grandparents as long as none of them are over the income limits.

Finally, the new law allows corporations and other entities such as tax-exempt organizations to make contributions to Education IRAs after 2001. There are no income limitations for nonindividual contributors.

QUALIFIED EDUCATION EXPENSES. The new law broadens the reach of Education IRAs beyond higher education costs by also allowing tax-free distributions after 2001 for expenses of kindergarten through high school. This includes private and religious elementary and secondary school costs as well as public school costs. Computer equipment, educational software, Internet access, tutoring, and the funding of qualified tuition programs (which

are discussed in the next section) are qualified elementary and secondary education expenses, as well as tuition, fees, books, supplies, equipment, room and board, uniforms, transportation, and extended day programs.

In order to more properly reflect the actual costs of higher education, the $2,500 limitation for off-campus room and board expenses has been removed for years after 2001. This expense is now limited to the amount allocated to room and board by the institution in its calculation of a student's costs of attendance for federal financial aid programs. Students living on campus can treat the actual invoice amount charged for room and board as a qualifying higher education expense.

SPECIAL NEEDS CHILDREN. Education IRAs for children with special needs have been provided an increased flexibility. Generally, contributions to Education IRAs must cease at age 18 and the account must be emptied by age 30. After 2001, these deadlines will not apply to special needs students. The IRS will have to issue regulations defining what a "special needs beneficiary" is. Congress wants the IRS to define the term as applying to an individual who, because of a physical, mental, or emotional condition (including a learning disability) requires additional time to complete his or her education.

Section 529 Qualified Tuition Plans

State-sponsored tuition plans, commonly called qualified state tuition plans (QSTPs) or Section 529 plans (after the section of the Internal Revenue Code that provides the tax rules for such plans), allow individuals to invest in prepaid tuition programs or contribute to state-managed higher education savings accounts. The new law provides more favorable tax treatment to qualified distributions and allows private colleges to set up qualified tuition plans.

Pre-2001 Tax Act

TYPES OF PLANS. Traditionally, Section 529 plans are established and maintained by a state and allow participants to prepay college tuition at the current rate, regardless of how much it increases in the interim, or to contribute to a higher education savings account.

Large amounts (in excess of $100,000, in some states) can be invested into a qualified tuition plan. Investment management is turned over to the state or to an investment firm hired by the state. Many state plans offer in-state investors a deduction or credit against their state income tax. Several state-sponsored qualified tuition plans are open to out-of-state residents as well as in-state residents and permit account funds to be used at virtually any accredited school in the United States, including private colleges.

DISTRIBUTIONS. Earnings on prepayments or contributions accumulate tax free within the state plan until withdrawn. The beneficiary is taxed on the earnings when distributions are made to pay for the beneficiary's qualified higher education expenses: tuition, fees, books, supplies, equipment, and room and board (limited to $2,500 for students living off campus). If a plan withdrawal is not used to pay qualifying higher education costs, or a refund is made to a contributor for a reason other than the beneficiary's receipt of a scholarship, or disability or death of the beneficiary, the state plan must impose a monetary penalty on the earnings portion of the distribution.

ROLLOVER OPTION. Participants have the option to roll over the account balance of one student to another student's account if the transferee is a family member of the former beneficiary. This rollover is tax- and penalty-free.

New Law

PRIVATE COLLEGE PLANS. Starting in 2002, private colleges and universities may establish a qualified tuition plan (QTP) that offers prepaid tuition. Private QTP prepaid tuition plans must hold the plan assets in a

TIP

Parents or grandparents can give up to $50,000 to qualified tuition plans and elect to have that gift spread over five years, for gift tax purposes. Such gifts therefore qualify for the $10,000 annual gift tax exclusion.

trust that has been approved by the IRS. Private educational institutions may offer only prepaid educational services and not education savings accounts.

As under pre-2001 Tax Act rules, a state-maintained QTP may provide either type of plan.

> **TIP**
>
> **Distributions from the eligible private education institution plans are not treated as tax-free until 2004.**

DISTRIBUTIONS. Starting in 2002, withdrawals from a *state-maintained* plan will be tax-free to the extent used for qualified higher education expenses. The exclusion from income applies to in-kind distributions from prepaid plans, such as tuition waivers as well as cash distributions from savings account QTPs. Similar to the Education IRA, the $2,500 limitation for off-campus room and board expenses will not apply after 2001. The definition of "qualified higher education expenses" will include the amount of room and board allocated to the student by the institution in its calculation of a student's costs of attendance for federal financial aid programs.

> **TIP**
>
> **After 2001, qualified higher education expenses include the expenses of a special needs beneficiary that are necessary in the student's enrollment or attendance at school.**

Distributions from qualifying *private* prepaid tuition programs that are made after 2004 will be eligible for the exclusion. As noted earlier, such private prepaid programs cannot be established until 2002.

Starting in 2002, the new law imposes a 10 percent penalty on taxable withdrawals from qualified tuition plans, which will come into play if earnings are withdrawn and not spent on education. This brings the QTP in line with the Education IRAs, which are subjected to a similar penalty.

A special penalty exception applies in 2002 and 2003 to certain distributions from QTPs of private educational institutions. Before 2004, when the exclusion for private QTPs becomes available, a distribution allocable to earnings is taxable even if used to pay qualified higher education expenses, but the 10 percent penalty won't be imposed on the earnings portion so used.

> **TIP**
>
> If an emergency arises and you need some cash, it can be withdrawn from a qualified tuition plan, at the risk of a penalty. However, if the money is not needed for college because of the beneficiary's death or disability, penalty-free withdrawals are permitted.

ROLLOVER OPTION. The list of qualified family members to which a plan can be rolled over (within 60 days) has been expanded to include any first cousins of the beneficiary. Further, the new law allows participants to roll over the QTP account of a plan beneficiary to another QTP for the same beneficiary, tax-free. Both rollover options are effective starting in 2002.

It should be noted that tax-free rollovers for the same

Example

The Joneses have been putting money into a state plan for the past two years in order to save for Billy's education. Some exciting promotional pieces convince the Joneses that a private prepaid tuition plan is a better option. After 2001, the Joneses can roll over the amount in the state plan into the private plan (or vice versa).

Unless Congress renews the provision permitting tax-free withdrawals from qualified tuition plans, the provision will expire after 2010, along with all other 2001 Tax Act provisions that are not renewed by the end of 2010.

Does this mean you should avoid investing in a QTP for a young child who'll enter college after 2010? Not necessarily. Even if this law is annulled, qualified tuition plans will revert to the pre-2001 Act law, so withdrawals of earnings would be taxed at the student's presumably low tax rate.

beneficiary can be done only once every 12 months. The 12-month rule does not apply to rollovers for the benefit of another family member.

College Education Deductions

For years there has been a good amount of lip service paid to the idea of making education more affordable. One such method would be to make the expenses deductible—much like mortgage interest. In this tax bill, we begin to see some limited movement in this direction.

Pre-2001 Tax

Under the pre-2001 Tax Act rules, individual taxpayers generally cannot deduct their (or their dependents') educational expenses. There is an exception for certain educational expenses relating to the taxpayer's current job. There is no deduction for the cost of an undergraduate education or other costs that qualify an individual for a new trade or business. Deductible employee expenses are included only as a miscellaneous itemized deduction—meaning that the taxpayer must itemize his or her deductions to gain any benefit and that the expenses can be taken only to the extent they plus other miscellaneous expenses exceed 2 percent of adjusted gross income.

New Law

The new tax law generally allows taxpayers whose incomes do not exceed a phaseout limit to deduct a portion of their qualified higher education expenses whether they itemize their deductions or not (often termed an "above-the-line" deduction). Thus, the 2 percent adjusted gross income requirement does not apply.

> **TIP**
>
> In general, qualified higher education expenses consist of tuition and fees paid to an eligible educational institution.

The deduction is scheduled to last for only four years, from 2002 through 2005. Unless Congress extends it, the deduction will not be available after 2005.

The amount of the deduction and income phaseout is outlined in Table 3.1. It should be noted that these are "cliff" deductions, meaning that you fall off without a net. For example, if your MAGI on a joint return is $130,000 or less in 2002, you can take a $3,000 deduction for college expenses you incur. If your MAGI is $130,001, you get no deduction.

These deductions may *not* be claimed by:

- Married couples who file separate returns.
- Taxpayers who can be claimed as dependents on another taxpayer's return.

A good rule of thumb for taxes is that you cannot get a double tax benefit for the same expenses. The education deduction rules guard against just such a situation. The deduction may *not* be claimed if a Hope or Lifetime Learning

TABLE 3.1 College Education Deduction Income Limits and Phaseout

TAX YEARS	MODIFIED ADJUSTED GROSS INCOME	MAXIMUM AMOUNT DEDUCTIBLE
2002 and 2003	Not more than $65,000 (unmarried) or $130,000 (married filing jointly)	$3,000
	More than $65,000 (unmarried) or $130,000 (married filing jointly)	None
2004 and 2005	Not more than $65,000 (unmarried) or $130,000 (married filing jointly)	$4,000
	More than $65,000 but not more than $80,000 (unmarried), or more than $130,000 but not more than $160,000 (married filing jointly)	$2,000
	More than $80,000 (unmarried) or $160,000 (married filing jointly)	None

credit is claimed for the same student in the same year. Also, the deduction may not be claimed for expenses taken into account when figuring tax-free interest on U.S. savings bonds used to pay tuition. If a distribution is received from an Education IRA, the tax-free portion of the distribution reduces the expenses eligible for the deduction. For Section 529 qualified tuition plan distributions, there is a twist: The new higher education deduction may be claimed for the

Example 1

Don withdraws $1,300 from his Education IRA in 2002 to pay for qualified higher education costs. Of this $1,300, $900 represents the original investment and $400 represents the earnings. Don would not pay any tax on the withdrawal because the distribution does not exceed qualified education expenses. Since the $1,300 distribution is tax-free, Don would be prohibited from taking a deduction for the $1,300 of expenses paid for with that money.

Example 2

Same scenario as Example 1, but the withdrawal is made from a qualified state tuition plan. Again, Don would not owe any tax on the withdrawal under the new law that allows an exclusion for qualifying distributions from a state-maintained QTP after 2001. However, the $900 return of contributions would support an educational deduction for $900 of higher education expenses (assuming he meets the income limits).

portion of a Section 529 plan distribution that represents a tax-free return of contributions.

Educational Assistance Plans

Educational assistance plans (EAPs) are offered to employees as fringe benefits by their employers. The advantage to employees is that EAP benefits may be tax-free.

The new law expands EAP benefits and makes them permanent.

EAPs come with strings attached from the employer's point of view. A plan must be written and must not discriminate in favor of highly compensated employees. No more than 5 percent of the amount paid each year can go to owners with at least a 5 percent stake in the company.

Pre-2001 Tax Act

The maximum amount employees are allowed to exclude from income under EAPs is limited to $5,250 annually and applies only to undergraduate-level courses. The exclusion for undergraduate costs expires for courses starting after 2001.

TIP

EAPs can't pay for the education of spouses or dependents.

New Law

The expiration of the EAP in 2002 has been repealed, making the benefit permanent. Further, EAPs are expanded to include graduate-level courses beginning in 2002. Unfortunately, the $5,250 limitation remains unchanged.

TIP

If you're an employer, consider creating an EAP to encourage your employees to further their educations.

Coordination of the Education Incentives

One of the more perplexing aspects of these education incentives is determining how they function together. There are six programs that must be considered: the Education IRA, qualified tuition programs, college education deductions, employer-assisted plans, the Hope Scholarship credit, and the Lifetime Learning credit. We've not discussed the Hope and the Lifetime Learning credits thus far because the new tax law does not directly affect them.

A quick review of the Hope and Lifetime Learning credits follows.

HOPE SCHOLARSHIP CREDIT. This is a per-student credit, available for the first two years of education after high school. The maximum credit is $1,500 per student per year, as long as at least $2,000 is spent on each student's tuition and fees in the year.

> **Example**
>
> Jill and Bob Smith have three children: twin sons and an older daughter. The sons are college freshmen, and the daughter is a sophomore. The Smiths can claim Hope Scholarship credits for all three students—up to $4,500 per year.

LIFETIME LEARNING CREDIT. This is a per-taxpayer credit. It provides for a 20 percent credit on the money spent on post-secondary tuition and related fees, up to $5,000 per year—meaning that the credit is limited to $1,000 per year. The $1,000 limit applies regardless of how many students incur education expenses. The Lifetime Learning credit covers virtually any learning expense that helps the student acquire new skills or improve old ones.

> **TIP**
>
> You can't use the Hope and Lifetime Learning credits for the same student in the same year.

> **Example**
>
> Jill and Bob Smith have three children: twin sons and an older daughter. The sons are college freshmen, and the daughter is a sophomore. The Smiths' qualified expenses total $15,000 per year, but they will be able to claim only $1,000 in total for the Lifetime Learning credit per year.

PHASEOUT OF CREDITS. To get the full Hope or Lifetime Learning credits, your modified adjusted gross income must be

If you can't use these credits because of income limits, your child may be eligible. Even though you can claim your child as your dependent, IRS regulations say that you can forgo a dependency exemption and let your child claim the credit. You may find that allowing your child to claim the credit provides a larger tax savings than a dependency exemption for the child, especially if your income is high enough to trigger a partial phaseout of the deduction for exemptions.

under $80,000 on a joint return ($40,000 if not married). Both credits phase out for modified adjusted gross income between $40,000 and $50,000, or $80,000 and $100,000 if married filing jointly.

Education IRAs and Education Credits

Under pre-2001 Tax Act rules, neither the Hope nor the Lifetime Learning credit can be claimed for the expenses of a student who, in the same year, receives a tax-free withdrawal from an Education IRA. However, if the student waives tax-free treatment and pays tax on the Education IRA distribution, a credit could be claimed.

Starting in 2002, tax-free distributions from an Education IRA can be received in the same year that a Hope or Lifetime Learning credit is claimed, provided the credit and the exclusion are not used for the same expenses for the same student. Expenses taken into account for purposes of the Hope or Lifetime Learning credit reduce "qualified education expenses" for the student in figuring excludable Education IRA distributions.

Example 1

Suppose it costs $20,000 to pay for daughter Betty's senior-year tuition and fees at college in 2002. If you decide to use the Lifetime Learning credit of $1,000 (thus covering $5,000 worth of the expenses) you will be limited to using only $15,000 from her Education IRA to pay for the other costs.

Example 2

Assume the same scenario, but you decide to pay for all of the $20,000 worth of expenses from the Education IRA. This will preclude you from using either the Lifetime Learning credit or the Hope credit.

Contributions to Education IRAs and Qualified Tuition Plans

The new law repeals the 6 percent excise tax that applied to an Education IRA contribution if any contributions were made to a QTP on behalf of the same beneficiary during the same year.

Qualified Tuition Programs, Education IRAs, and Education Credits

Under the new law, QTP and Education IRA distributions can be used in the same year as a Hope or Lifetime Learning credit. Again, this is reliant on the fact that they are not used for the same expenses for the same student. For purposes of figuring how much of the QTP and/or Education IRA distributions can be excluded from income, "qualified expenses" are reduced first by tax-free scholarships and then by expenses taken into account when figuring the Hope or Lifetime Learning credit.

If distributions from both an Education IRA and a QTP are received in the same year, and the total distributions from both plans exceed the "qualified expenses" as reduced by the expenses used for education credits, the expenses will have to be allocated between the QTP and Education IRA distributions.

College Tuition Education Deductions

As discussed earlier in this chapter, taxpayers cannot claim the new above-the-line deduction for higher education tuition and related fees if a Hope or Lifetime Learning credit is claimed in the same year for the student. To avoid a double benefit, expenses eligible for the deduction are reduced by tax-free distributions from an Education IRA, tax-free interest from U.S. Savings Bonds used for tuition, and tax-free distributions from qualified tuition plans that are allocable to earnings.

Coverage by Educational Assistance Plans

The various educational incentives of the new tax law are all predicated on the fact that the taxpayer is offsetting an educational expense. If this expense is actually paid by the taxpayer's employer, there is no expense to offset. Thus, none of the incentives can be used for educational

Effective in 2002, it will be possible to contribute to an Education IRA and a qualified tuition plan for the same student in the same year. One strategy, then, is to fund an Education IRA first, up to $2,000 per year, and then put what you can into a qualified tuition plan.

Why put your first dollars into an Education IRA? Because Education IRAs are self-directed while qualified tuition plans compel you to turn the money over to a state-run investment pool. The money you put into an Education IRA can go into stocks, which are likely to produce higher long-term returns than the balanced portfolios of many qualified tuition plans.

expenses that are covered by educational assistance plans.

Example

Your son Joe pays $5,000 for a computer course for which he is reimbursed by his employer under an EAP. Joe can exclude that $5,000 from his income—but he can't use that same $5,000 as the basis for a Lifetime Learning credit.

Student Loans

Since 1998, a limited amount of student loan interest has been deductible. The new tax law makes the deduction available to more individuals by liberalizing the income phaseout rules and eliminating the time limit for claiming the deduction.

Pre-2001 Tax Act

SIZE OF DEDUCTION. The interest on a student loan (for yourself, for a spouse, or for a dependent) is deductible up to $2,500 per year. The deduction may *not* be claimed by an individual who can be claimed as a dependent by another taxpayer, or by married persons filing separately.

PERIOD WHEN DEDUCTION IS AVAILABLE. Deductions are permitted only for the first 60 months of the payback period.

INCOME LIMITATIONS. The deduction is available for taxpayers with modified adjusted gross incomes (MAGI) under $40,000 ($60,000 for joint filers). The amount of the deduction is then phased out until it is completely unavailable for those with MAGI of $55,000 ($75,000 for joint filers) or more.

REQUIRED PAYMENTS. Only interest payments that are required to be paid are deductible. This means that if an interest payment is made during a period of forbearance, for example, it will not be deductible because the payment is not considered to be required.

New Law

PERIOD WHEN DEDUCTION IS AVAILABLE. The 2001 Tax Act eliminates the 60-month limitation for student loan interest paid after 2001. This will enable those who were prevented from

> ### Example
>
> Sally began making payments on her loan in 1994. Her 60-month period ended in 1999, and therefore she was not allowed to take a deduction for her interest payments beyond that year. Now, in 2002, Sally will be able to take a deduction for her interest payments on the same loan—for the remaining life of the loan. (Note that Sally cannot file an amended return and take deductions for 2000 and 2001.)

deducting student loan interest before 2002, because of the 60-month limitation, to deduct interest payments they make on the same loan after 2001.

INCOME LIMITATIONS. The income limitations have been raised. Now, for years after 2001, the phaseout range for unmarried taxpayers will begin at $50,000, while for joint filers it will begin at $100,000. The deduction will be completely eliminated at $65,000 and $130,000, respectively.

REQUIRED PAYMENTS. The new law has eliminated the required payment provision. Thus all interest payments, even those made in forbearance, will be eligible for the deduction.

Scholarships under the National Health Service Corps and the Armed Forces Health Professions Programs

In general, college or university degree candidates don't have to include amounts received through qualified scholarships in their taxable income. However, tax-free treatment is not allowed for scholarships that require recipients to provide services, as the scholarships are deemed to represent payment for those services.

Pre-2001 Tax Act

Under the restriction just listed, tax-free treatment does not apply to any amount received by a student that represents payments for teaching, research, or other services performed as a condition for receiving the scholarship or tuition reduction. This includes federal grants requiring future medical services of recipients of the National Health Service Corps Scholarship program and the Armed Forces Health Professions Scholarship and Financial Assistance program.

New Law

Starting in 2002, payments to degree candidates for tuition, fees, books, supplies, and equipment under the National Health Service Corps Scholarship program and the Armed Forces Health Professions Scholarship and Financial Assistance program will be tax-free, despite the fact that there is a future service obligation.

CHAPTER 4

Estate, Gift, and Generation-Skipping Transfer Tax Relief*

The slow phase-in of the estate tax repeal, fully effective in 2010, together with the sunset of all provisions of the Act in 2011 means that the estate tax repeal will be in effect, barring Congressional action, for only one year (2010). This makes tax planning very difficult. While it is unlikely that Congress will allow the entire Tax Act to sunset, it is hard to know what the future of the estate tax will be. Readers should be alert to the possibility that the estate tax may return, at least in some form, after 2010.

*Without an act of Congress, all of the new laws enacted by the 2001 Tax Act will disappear (or "sunset") at the end of 2010, and the rules in effect prior to the 2001 Tax Act will again be law. See the Introduction for more details.

Phaseout and Repeal of the Estate Tax and Generation-Skipping Tax; Modification of the Gift Tax

Pre-2001 Tax Act

TAX RATES. A gift tax is imposed on transfers of a person's assets while the person is alive, and an estate tax is imposed on transfers at death. The gift tax and the estate tax are unified, so that a single graduated rate schedule applies to the total amount of taxable transfers made by a taxpayer during his or her lifetime and at death.

> **TIP**
>
> There is an annual exclusion for gifts of $10,000 and under.

The unified estate and gift tax rates begin at 18 percent on the first $10,000 of cumulative taxable transfers and reach 55 percent on cumulative taxable transfers over $3 million. (See Table 4.1.)

In addition to the schedule in Table 4.1, there is a 5 percent surcharge imposed on transfers between $10 million and $17,184,000. Thus, these estates are subject to a top marginal rate of 60 percent. Estates over $17,184,000 are subject to a flat rate of 55 percent.

A special estate tax deduction may be allowed for a family-owned business. Up to $675,000 of the adjusted value of the business may be deductible, and the deduction, together with the annual exclusion amount, may shield up to $1.3 million of family business assets from the estate tax in 2001.

TABLE 4.1 Unified Gift and Estate Tax Rates—Pre-2001 Tax Act

IF TAXABLE AMOUNT IS OVER:	BUT NOT OVER:	THE TAX IS:	PLUS:	OF THE AMOUNT OVER:
$ 0	$ 10,000	$ 0	18%	$ 0
$ 10,000	$ 20,000	$ 1,800	20%	$ 10,000
$ 20,000	$ 40,000	$ 3,800	22%	$ 20,000
$ 40,000	$ 60,000	$ 8,200	24%	$ 40,000
$ 60,000	$ 80,000	$ 13,000	26%	$ 60,000
$ 80,000	$ 100,000	$ 18,200	28%	$ 80,000
$ 100,000	$ 150,000	$ 23,800	30%	$ 100,000
$ 150,000	$ 250,000	$ 38,800	32%	$ 150,000
$ 250,000	$ 500,000	$ 70,800	34%	$ 250,000
$ 500,000	$ 750,000	$ 155,800	37%	$ 500,000
$ 750,000	$1,000,000	$ 248,300	39%	$ 750,000
$1,000,000	$1,250,000	$ 345,800	41%	$1,000,000
$1,250,000	$1,500,000	$ 448,300	43%	$1,250,000
$1,500,000	$2,000,000	$ 555,800	45%	$1,500,000
$2,000,000	$2,500,000	$ 780,800	49%	$2,000,000
$2,500,000	$3,000,000	$1,025,800	53%	$2,500,000
$3,000,000		$1,290,800	55%	$3,000,000

UNIFIED CREDIT. Estates of individuals dying after 1997 are entitled to a unified credit that generally shields assets transferred from the estate tax. See Table 4.2 for the unified credit schedule as outlined in the pre-2001 Tax Act law.

TABLE 4.2 Unified Credit Schedule—Pre-2001 Tax Act

YEAR OF DEATH	EXEMPTION AMOUNT	UNIFIED CREDIT
1998	$ 625,000	$202,050
1999	$ 650,000	$211,300
2000-2001	$ 675,000	$220,550
2002-2003	$ 700,000	$229,800
2004	$ 850,000	$287,300
2005	$ 950,000	$326,300
2006 and thereafter	$1,000,000	$345,800

Example

Jim is an unmarried person who made no taxable gifts after 1976. He dies in 2001, leaving a gross estate of $700,000. Debts, administration costs, and funeral expenses total $60,000. He bequeaths $160,000 to charity. After deductions and credits, no estate tax will be due.

Gross estate	$700,000
Less funeral and other expenses	($60,000)
	$640,000
Less charitable bequest	($160,000)
Taxable estate	$480,000
Tentative tax	$149,000
Less unified credit	($220,550)
Estate tax	0

GENERATION-SKIPPING TAX. A generation-skipping transfer tax (GST tax) generally is imposed on transfers that skip a generation, such as a gift to a grandchild, if it exceeds a lifetime exemption of $1.6 million (the amount for 2001) per transferor, subject to inflation adjustments. The generation-skipping transfer tax is imposed at a flat rate of 55 percent.

New Law

The estate tax exemption will be increased and the top marginal estate tax rate will be reduced in stages from 2002 through 2009. The estate tax (and generation-skipping tax) will then be repealed for estates of individuals dying after 2009. Gift tax rates before 2010 will be the same as the estate tax rates, but exemption amounts will be different after 2003. The gift tax will be retained with modifications when the estate tax is repealed in 2010.

Note the caveat in estate tax repeal: the entire 2001 Tax Act, including the estate tax repeal provision, will expire in 2011 unless Congress acts to make the provisions permanent. If Congress does not extend the provisions or make other changes, the pre-2001 Act estate tax rules will apply in 2011, with a $1 million exemption and a top tax rate of 55%.

ESTATE TAX RATES AND EXEMPTION. From 2002 through 2009, the estate and gift tax rates and unified credit amounts are gradually reduced and exemption amounts are increased (see Table 4.3). In 2002, the 5 percent surcharge on estates between $10 million and $17,184,000 and rates in excess of 50 percent are repealed. Until the repeal of the estate tax in 2010, pre-Act deductions such as the unlimited marital deduction and charitable deduction will generally continue to apply. However, starting in 2004, the family-owned business deduction as described above is repealed.

TIP

The gift tax was retained so that taxpayers could not utilize gifts as a tool to avoid income taxes.

GIFT TAX. The new law does not change the $10,000 annual per donee gift tax exclusion ($20,000 for split gifts of married couples), indexed for infla-

TABLE 4.3 Phasedown and Repeal of the Estate Tax

YEAR	ESTATE AND GST TAX EXEMPTION AMOUNT	HIGHEST ESTATE AND GIFT TAX RATES
2002	$1 million	50%
2003	$1 million	49%
2004	$1.5 million	48%
2005	$1.5 million	47%
2006	$2 million	46%
2007	$2 million	45%
2008	$2 million	45%
2009	$3.5 million	45%
2010	Total repeal of estate tax and GST tax. The exemption for gift tax purposes remains at $1 million as increased in 2002. Top gift tax rate after 2009 will equal the prevailing top personal income tax rate, scheduled to be 35 percent under the 2001 Act.	

tion. Starting in 2002, a lifetime gift tax exemption of $1 million will apply. The exemption will stay at $1 million and not increase when the estate tax exemption increases above $1 million after 2003. The rates for gift tax and estate tax or 2002–2009 are the same. See Table 4.3 for the scheduled reductions to the top rate. Beginning in 2010, the top gift tax rate will be the same as the top individual income tax rate scheduled to be 35%. Further, transfers to a trust will be treated as a taxable gift, unless the trust is treated as wholly owned by the donor or the donor's spouse.

GENERATION-SKIPPING TAX. The 2001 Act repeals the generation-skipping transfer tax after 2009. Because of the complexity of these rules, you should consult an experienced tax practitioner if you are planning a "skip" transfer to determine if and how the generation-skipping tax rules apply to you.

Reduction in State Death Tax Credit; Deduction for State Death Taxes Paid

The estate of a decedent is entitled to a federal credit for any state death taxes paid. The 2001 Tax Act generally reduces the amount of the credit, eventually changing it to a deduction, and then removing it altogether, along with the estate tax.

Pre-2001 Tax Act

A credit is allowed against the federal estate tax for state death taxes. The maximum amount of credit allowable is determined under a graduated rate table, the top rate of

TIP

Most states impose a "soak-up" estate tax, which serves to impose a state tax equal to the maximum federal credit allowed.

which is 16 percent, based on the size of the decedent's adjusted taxable estate.

New Law

The credit for state death taxes will be reduced between 2002 and 2004. It will be completely repealed for the estates of people dying after 2004. At that point, the credit will be changed to a deduction until the phaseout of the federal estate tax is complete.

From 2002 to 2004, the state death tax credit is reduced as follows:

Year	Reduction
2002	25%
2003	50%
2004	75%
2005	state death tax credit is repealed, after which there will be a deduction for death taxes actually paid with respect to property included in the gross estate.

Basis of Property Acquired from Decedent

Under pre-2001 Tax Act law, the basis of property acquired from a decedent is generally the fair market value of the

Deductible state death taxes will include any estate, inheritance, legacy, or succession taxes, imposed by any state or the District of Columbia. Such state taxes must have been paid and claimed before the later of: (1) four years after the filing of the estate tax return, (2) 60 days after the final decision of the Tax Court determining the estate tax liability, (3) the expiration of the period of extension to pay estate taxes over time, (4) the expiration of the period of limitations in which to file a claim for refund, or (5) 60 days after a decision of a court in which such refund suit had become final.

property at the time of the decedent's death. With the repeal of the estate tax, as provided by the 2001 Tax Act, the basis rules have been modified.

Pre-2001 Tax Act

Gain or loss on the sale of property is measured by the amount realized on the disposition, less the taxpayer's basis in the property. Basis generally represents a taxpayer's investment in the property, with certain adjustments. For example, basis is increased by the cost of capital improvements made to the property and decreased by depreciation deductions taken with respect to the property.

In the case of property passing from a decedent's estate, the basis in the property will generally be stepped up. Stepped-up basis, for estate tax purposes, means that the

Example

Lonny and Darlene purchased their home in 1965 for $56,000. They sold the home in 2000 for $256,000. Over the years, they had made some improvements to the property in the amount of $15,000. Therefore, at the time of the sale, their basis in the property was $71,000 ($56,000 + $15,000). Their gain on the property was $185,000 ($256,000 – $71,000).

basis of property passing from a decedent's estate generally is the fair market value on the date of the decedent's death (or, if the alternate valuation date is elected, the earlier of six months after the decedent's death or the date the property is sold or distributed by the estate).

Example

Lonny has owned a collectible watch for many years. He leaves the watch to Sue in his will. At the time of his death, the watch (for which he paid $4,000) is worth $15,000. Sue's basis in the watch will be $15,000.

New Law

Starting in 2010, the rules providing for a fair market value basis in property acquired from a decedent (the step-up in basis as described in the preceding section) are repealed. Instead, a modified carryover basis regime generally takes effect. Recipients of property transferred at the decedent's death will receive a basis equal to the adjusted basis of the property in the hands of the decedent or the fair market value of the property on the date of the decedent's death—whichever is lower.

The modified carryover basis rules apply to property acquired by bequest, devise, or inheritance, or by the decedent's estate from the decedent; property passing from the decedent to the extent such property passed without consideration, and certain other property to which the prior law stepped-up basis rules applied.

Example

George received a bequest of property from his uncle's estate in 2010. The property had a fair market value of $100,000 on the date of his uncle's death. George's uncle had an adjusted basis of $50,000 in the property. George's basis in the property under the pre-2001 Tax Act law would have been $100,000 (the fair market value on the date of decedent's death). Under the new law, George's basis will be $50,000—the lesser of the adjusted basis of the uncle ($50,000) or the fair market value on the date of death ($100,000) unless the executor increases the basis under the exception to the carryover basis rule discussed in the next section.

Had the fair market value of the property been $40,000, George's basis would have been $40,000.

> Property acquired from a decedent is treated as if the property had been acquired by gift. Thus, the character of the gain on the sale of property received from a decedent's estate is carried over to the heir. For example, real estate that has been depreciated and would be subject to recapture if sold by the decedent will be subject to recapture if sold by the heir.

Basis Increase for Certain Property

After 2009, the 2001 Tax Act allows the executor of an estate to step-up within limits the basis of the assets within the estate. This provision is designed to provide some relief from the repeal of stepped-up basis rules after 2009, discussed in the preceding section.

Pre-2001 Tax Act

Property passing from a decedent's estate generally takes a stepped-up basis (described earlier in the chapter).

New Law

The new law provides a modified carryover basis for assets acquired from a decedent after 2009 (as described previously). But, beginning in 2010, an executor may increase (i.e., step-up) the basis in assets owned

TIP

The basis of property transferred after 2009 to surviving spouses can be increased by a total of $4.3 million.

by the decedent and acquired by the beneficiaries at death. Under this rule, the executor of each decedent's estate generally is permitted to increase (i.e., step-up) the basis of assets transferred by up to a total of $1.3 million. (The $1.3 million limit is increased by the amount of unused capital losses, net operating losses, and certain built-in losses of the decedent.) In addition, the basis of property transferred to a surviving spouse can be increased by an additional $3 million.

Executors of estates of nonresidents who are not U.S. citizens will be allowed to increase the basis of property by up to $60,000. The $60,000, $1.3 million, and $3 million amounts will be adjusted annually for inflation after 2010.

RULES APPLICABLE TO BASIS INCREASE. Basis increase will be allocable on an asset-by-asset basis (e.g., basis increase can be allocated to a share of stock or a block of stock). However, in no case can the basis of an asset be adjusted above its fair market value. If the amount of basis increase is less than the fair market value of assets eligible for the increase under these rules, the executor will determine which assets receive basis increases and to what extent each asset does so.

PROPERTY ELIGIBLE FOR BASIS INCREASE. Generally, the basis of property may be increased above the decedent's adjusted basis in that property only if the property is owned, or is treated as owned, by the decedent at the time of the decedent's death. In the case of property held as joint tenants or tenants by the entireties with the surviving spouse, one-half of the property is treated as having been owned by the decedent and is eligible for the basis increase. In the case of property held jointly with a person other than the surviving spouse, the portion of the property that the decedent had

Example 1

Lonny dies in 2010. His estate consists solely of shares in ABC company that have a fair market value of $8.5 million and a basis of $1.5 million. Lonny bequeaths all of this stock to his surviving spouse, Darlene. Lonny's executor can increase the basis in the stock to $5.8 million ($1.5 million basis + $1.3 million general basis increase + $3 million spousal property basis increase). Had Darlene not been alive at the time and had Lonny chosen to leave all of the stock to Fred, his son, the executor would have only been able to increase the basis to $2.8 million ($1.5 million + $1.3 million).

Example 2

Assume the same facts except that the fair market value of the stock is only $2 million. In this situation, the executor will only be able to increase the basis in the shares by $500,000, to $2 million. The executor is not able to increase the basis above the fair market value.

Example 3

Lonny's estate consists of property with a fair market value of $8.5 million. The basis in this property is $1 million. The estate also has stock with a fair market value of $4 million and a basis of $2 million. Since a full basis step-up ($9.5 million) would exceed the general basis increase ($1.3 million), Lonny's executor will decide how to use the general basis increase.

purchased is treated as having been owned by the decedent and will be eligible for a basis increase.

The decedent also is treated as the owner of property (which will be eligible for a basis increase) if the property was transferred by the decedent during his or her lifetime to a revocable trust in which the decedent receives all of its income during his or her life or, if not, has control over who receives the income. The decedent also is treated as having owned the surviving spouse's one-half share of community property (which will be eligible for a basis increase) if at least one-half of the property was owned by, and acquired from, the decedent.

TIP

Both the decedent's and the surviving spouse's share of community property could be eligible for a basis increase.

The decedent is not, however, treated as owning any property solely by reason of holding a power of appointment with respect to such property.

PROPERTY NOT ELIGIBLE FOR BASIS INCREASE. Property not available for the basis step-up includes: (1) property that was acquired by the decedent by gift (other than from his or her spouse) during the three-year period ending on the date of the decedent's death; (2) property that constitutes a right to receive income in respect of a decedent; (3) stock or securities of a foreign personal holding company; (4) stock of a domestic international sales corporation (or former domestic international sales corporation); (5) stock of a foreign investment company; and (6) stock of a passive foreign investment company (except for which a decedent shareholder has made a qualified electing fund election).

Income Tax Exclusion for the Gain on the Sale of a Principal Residence

Starting in 2010 the exclusion for gain on the sale of a principal residence will be extended to cover the sale of a residence by an heir or a decedent's estate in certain circumstances.

Pre-2001 Tax Act

A taxpayer can generally exclude from income taxes up to $250,000 ($500,000 if married and filing a joint return) of gain realized on the sale or exchange of a principal residence. The exclusion is allowed each time a taxpayer sells or exchanges a principal residence that meets the eligibility requirement listed in the next paragraph. The selling of property under this law can be generally no more frequently than once every two years.

To be eligible, a taxpayer must have owned the residence and occupied it as a principal residence for at least two of the five years prior to the sale or exchange of the property.

Example

Sarah and David sold their house in 2000 for a gain of $400,000. Over the prior five years, it had been the principal residence only one year due to health circumstances. In this case they can exclude $250,000 (half of the $500,000 exclusion) from income. Thus, they must recognize $150,000 ($400,000 − $250,000) of gain on the sale.

A taxpayer who fails to meet these requirements by reason of a change of place of employment, health, or other unforeseen circumstances is able to exclude the portion of the $250,000 limit ($500,000 if married filing a joint return) equal to the fraction of two years that these requirements are met.

New Law

The income tax exclusion for the sale of a principal residence is extended to estates and heirs for years after 2009. If the decedent's estate, heir, or qualified revocable trust established by the decedent sells the decedent's principal residence, $250,000 of gain can be excluded on the sale of the residence, provided the decedent owned and used the property as a principal residence for two or more years during the five-year period prior to the sale. In addition, if an heir occupies the property as a principal residence, the decedent's period of ownership and occupancy of the property as a principal residence can be added to the heir's subsequent ownership and occupancy in determining whether the property was owned and occupied for two years as a principal residence.

Example 1

Helen dies in 2001 and her estate sells her principal residence. Helen had owned and occupied the residence for the two years before her death. Helen had an adjusted basis in the residence of $100,000, and the residence sold for $350,000. The estate may exclude the $250,000 of gain from the sale.

Example 2

Helen left her principal residence to her nephew. Helen had owned and occupied the residence for one year before her death. Her nephew occupied the residence for one year after Helen's death and then sold the residence for $350,000. The nephew's adjusted basis in the house was $100,000 (which was Helen's adjusted basis in the house). The nephew may exclude the $250,000 gain, since Helen's period of ownership and use may be added to the nephew's period of ownership and use.

Reporting Requirements

With the repeal of the estate tax after 2009, estates will no longer be required to file estate tax returns. The new information-reporting requirements will ensure that, in the absence of the estate tax and the estate tax return, taxpayers and the IRS can receive sufficient information such that basis in property received from a decedent is properly determined.

Pre-2001 Tax Act

Estate tax returns are required for estates that exceed the applicable exclusion amount for the year of death.

New Law

TRANSFERS AT DEATH. For estates of individuals dying after 2009, the executor of the estate (or in some cases, the trustee of a revocable trust) will have to file an information return with the IRS to report (1) transfers at death of noncash assets in excess of $1.3 million and (2) appreciated property received from the decedent that the decedent acquired within three years of death, as a gift which was reportable by the donor on a gift tax return. The report to the IRS must include:

- Name and taxpayer identification number of the recipient of the property.
- Accurate description of the property.
- Adjusted basis of the property in the hands of the decedent and its fair market value at the time of death.
- Decedent's holding period for the property.
- Sufficient information to determine whether any gain on the sale of the property would be treated as ordinary income.
- Amount of basis increase allocated to the property.
- Any other information required by IRS regulations.

Similar statements must also be provided for the recipients of the property.

TRANSFERS DURING LIFE. Donors who file gift tax returns after 2009 will be required to provide to recipients the information relating to the property (e.g., the fair market value and basis of the property) that was reported on the donor's gift tax return.

PENALTIES. The penalties for failing to properly report transfers are:

- Any donor required to provide to recipients of property by gift the information reported on the gift tax return who fails to do so is liable for a penalty of $50 for each failure.

- Any person required to report transfers at death of noncash assets in excess of $1.3 million in value who fails to do so is liable for a penalty of $10,000.

- Any person required to report to the IRS the transfer by a decedent of appreciated property acquired by the decedent within three years of death—for which a gift tax return was required to have been filed by the donor—who fails to do so is liable for a penalty of $500 for the failure to report such information to the IRS. There is also a penalty of $50 for each failure to report such information to a beneficiary.

> **TIP**
>
> **The penalty for failing to report a transfer may be excused by the IRS for reasonable cause.**

If any failure to report to the IRS or a beneficiary is due to intentional disregard of the rules, then the penalty is 5 percent of the fair market value of the property for which reporting was required, determined at the date of the decedent's death (for property passing at death) or determined at the time of the gift (for a lifetime gift).

Installment Payment of Estate Tax for Closely Held Businesses

In an effort to assist small, closely held businesses, the 2001 Tax Act expands the definition of a closely held business for estate tax purposes, thus increasing the availability of the installment election.

Pre-2001 Tax Act

The estate tax generally is due within nine months of a decedent's death. However, an executor may elect to defer for five years payments of estate tax attributable to an interest in a closely held business and then pay the tax in two or more installments (but no more than 10). An estate is eligible for payment of the estate tax in installments if the value of the decedent's interest in a closely held business exceeds 35 percent of the decedent's adjusted gross estate (i.e., the gross estate less certain deductions).

If the election is made, the estate may defer payment of principal and pay only interest for the first five years, followed by up to 10 annual installments of principal and interest.

A special 2 percent interest rate applies to the amount of deferred estate tax attributable to the first $1 million in taxable value of a closely held business. The $1 million amount is adjusted annually for in-

> **TIP**
>
> This provision effectively extends the time for paying estate tax by 14 years from the original due date of the estate tax.

Example

Assume estate tax is due in 2001. If interest only is paid each year for the first five years (2001 through 2005), and if 10 installments of both principal and interest are paid for the 10 years thereafter (2006 through 2015), then payment of estate tax would be extended by 14 years from the original due date in 2001.

flation occurring after 1998. The inflation-adjusted amount for 2001 is $1,060,000.

For purposes of these rules, an interest in a closely held business is: (1) an interest as a proprietor in a sole proprietorship, (2) an interest as a partner in a partnership carrying on a trade or business if 20 percent or more of the total capital interest of such partnership is included in the decedent's gross estate or the partnership had 15 or fewer partners, and (3) stock in a corporation carrying on a trade or business if 20 percent or more of the value of the voting stock of the corporation is included in the decedent's gross estate or such corporation had 15 or fewer shareholders. The decedent may own the interest directly or, in certain cases, ownership may be indirect, through a holding company.

If ownership is through a holding company, the stock must be non–readily tradable. If stock in a holding company is treated as business company stock for purposes of the installment payment provisions, the five-year deferral for principal and the 2 percent interest rate do not apply. The value of any interest in a closely held business does not include the value of that portion of such interest attributable to passive assets held by such business.

New Law

After 2001, the definition of a closely held business for purposes of installment payment of estate tax is expanded. The number of partners in a partnership and shareholders in a corporation that is considered a closely held business in which a decedent held an interest is increased from 15 to 45, and thus will qualify the estate for installment payment of estate tax.

Also, an estate of a decedent with an interest in a qualifying lending and financing business is eligible for installment payment of the estate tax. An estate with an interest in a qualifying lending and financing business that claims installment payment of estate tax must make installment payments of estate tax (which will include both principal and interest) relating to the interest in a qualifying lending and financing business over five years.

The installment payment provisions require that only the stock of holding companies, not that of operating subsidiaries, must be non–readily tradable in order to qualify for installment payment of the estate tax.

An estate with a qualifying property interest held through holding companies that claims installment payment of estate tax must make all installment payments of estate tax (which will include both principal and interest) relating to a qualifying property interest held through holding companies over five years.

Transfers to Foreign Trusts, Foreign Estates, and Nonresidents Who Are Not U.S. Citizens

Under pre-2001 Tax Act law, transfers (during life or at death) to foreign trusts or estates are treated as sales or exchanges of the property. The new tax law changes this to cause only transfers at death to be treated in this manner.

Pre-2001 Tax Act

A transfer (during life or at death) by a U.S. person to a foreign trust or estate generally is treated as a sale or exchange of the property for an amount equal to the fair market value of the transferred property. The amount of gain that must be recognized by the transferor is equal to the excess of the fair market value of the property transferred over the adjusted basis (for purposes of determining gain) of such property in the hands of the transferor.

This gain recognition rule does not apply to transfers to nonresident aliens.

Example

Max, a U.S. citizen, transfers property with a basis of $100,000 and a fair market value of $500,000 to a foreign trust. Max must recognize a gain of $400,000 ($500,000 – $100,000) on the transfer.

New Law

Beginning in 2010 a transfer by a U.S. citizen's estate (i.e., by a U.S. person at death) to a nonresident who is not a U.S. citizen is treated as a sale or exchange of property for an amount equal to the fair market value of the transferred property. The amount of gain that must be recognized by the transferor is equal to the excess of the fair market value of the property transferred less the adjusted basis of the property in the hands of the transferor.

Example

Assume that Max's transfer is in 2010 to a nonresident who is not a U.S. citizen. Under the new tax law, Max will not have to recognize any gain on the transfer. Had Max's estate transferred the property, then the same $400,000 of gain would have to be recognized by the estate.

Transfers of Property in Satisfaction of Pecuniary Bequest

The new tax law changes the way in which the gain on property transferred from an estate in satisfaction of a pecuniary bequest is calculated.

Pre-2001 Tax Act

Gain or loss is recognized on the transfer of property in satisfaction of a pecuniary bequest (i.e., a bequest of a specific dollar amount) to the extent that the fair market value of the property at the time of the transfer exceeds the basis of the property, which generally is the basis stepped up to the fair market value on the date of the decedent's death.

New Law

Starting in 2010 gain or loss on the transfer of property in satisfaction of a pecuniary bequest is recognized only to the extent that the fair market value of the property at the time of the transfer exceeds the fair market value of the property on the date of the decedent's death (not the property's carryover basis).

Example

Frank's cousin left him $75,000 in her will. The executor of the cousin's estate satisfied the bequest by transferring a rare gem to Frank worth $75,000 on the date of transfer, but only $70,000 on the date of death. Frank's cousin had an adjusted basis of $40,000 in the gem. Under the new law after 2009, the cousin's estate recognizes only $5,000 of gain—the difference between the fair market value at the time of death ($70,000) and the fair market value at the time of distribution ($75,000).

Expansion of Estate Tax Rule for Conservation Easements

The contribution of a conservation easement in real property is eligible for a charitable deduction provided that it is donated to a qualified charitable organization for the sole purpose of conservation. The 2001 Tax Act expands the property that qualifies for this provision.

Pre-2001 Tax Act

An executor can elect to exclude from the taxable estate 40 percent of the value of any land subject to a qualified conservation easement, up to certain maximum exclusions:

Year	Maximum Amount of Exclusion
2001	$400,000
2002 and thereafter	$500,000

The exclusion percentage is reduced by 2 percentage points for each percentage point (or fraction thereof) by

A qualified conservation easement is one that meets the following requirements: (1) the land is located within 25 miles of a metropolitan area, national park, or wilderness area, or within 10 miles of an urban national forest; (2) the land has been owned by the decedent or a member of the decedent's family at all times during the three-year period ending on the date of the decedent's death; and (3) a qualified conservation contribution—within the meaning of Section 170(h) of the Internal Revenue Code—of a qualified real property interest was granted by the decedent or a member of his or her family.

For purposes of the exclusion for qualified conservation easements, preservation of a historically important land area or a certified historic structure does not qualify as a conservation purpose.

Urban national forests are designated by the Forest Service of the U.S. Department of Agriculture. A metropolitan area is defined for these purposes by the Office of Management and Budget.

which the value of the qualified conservation easement is less than 30 percent of the value of the land (determined without regard to the value of such easement and reduced by the value of any retained development right).

In order to qualify for the exclusion, a qualifying easement must have been granted by the decedent, a member of the decedent's family, the executor of the decedent's estate, or the trustee of a trust holding the land, no later than the date of the election. To the extent that the value of such land is excluded from the taxable estate, the basis of such land acquired at death is a carryover basis (i.e., the basis is not stepped up to its fair market value at death). Property financed with acquisition indebtedness is eligible for this provision only to the extent of net equity in the property.

RETAINED DEVELOPMENT RIGHTS. The exclusion for land subject to a conservation easement does not apply to any development right retained by the donor in the conveyance of the conservation easement. An example of a development right would be the right to extract minerals from the land. The value of the conservation easement must be reduced by the value of any retained development right.

If the donor or holders of the development rights agree in writing to extinguish the development rights in the land, then the value of the easement need not be reduced by the development rights. In such a case, those persons with an interest in the land must execute the agreement no later than the earlier of (1) two years after the date of the decedent's death or (2) the date of the sale of such land subject to the conservation easement. If such agreement is not entered into within that time, then those with an interest in the land are personally liable for an additional tax, which is the amount of tax that would have been due on the retained development rights subject to the termination agreement.

New Law

After 2000, the availability of qualified conservation easements is expanded by eliminating the requirement that the land be located within a certain distance from a metropolitan area, national park, wilderness area, or urban national forest.

TIP

A qualified conservation easement may therefore be claimed with respect to any land that is located in the United States or its possessions.

The date for determining easement compliance is the date on which the donation was made.

Generation-Skipping Transfer Tax Rules

Transfers that skip a generation, such as a gift to a grandchild, are subject to a special tax if they exceed a lifetime exemption ($1,060,000 for 2001). The 2001 Tax Act makes several technical changes to the generation-skipping tax laws. Because of the complexity of these rules, you should consult an experienced tax practitioner if you have generation-skipping issues.

CHAPTER 5

Pension and Individual Retirement Arrangement Relief*

Individual Retirement Arrangements

Participation in individual retirement accounts (IRAs) by the American public has been lackluster. In an effort to combat this, the new tax law increases the maximum annual contribution to both traditional IRAs and Roth IRAs. The new limit will be increased over the next seven years until it reaches $5,000 in 2008. This amount will then be indexed for inflation for years thereafter.

---

*Without an act of Congress, all of the new laws enacted by the 2001 Tax Act will disappear (or "sunset") at the end of 2010 and the rules in effect prior to the 2001 Tax Act will again be law. See the Introduction for more details.

Pre-2001 Tax Act

There are two general types of individual retirement arrangements: traditional IRAs, to which both deductible and nondeductible contributions may be made, and Roth IRAs to which nondeductible contributions may be made.

TRADITIONAL IRAs. Deductible contributions to an IRA up to the lesser of $2,000 or the individual's compensation can be made if neither the individual nor the individual's spouse is an active participant in an employer-sponsored retirement plan. For married couples, deductible IRA contributions of up to $2,000 can be made for each spouse (including, for example, a homemaker who does not work outside the home), if the combined compensation of both spouses is at least equal to the contributed amount. If the individual (or the individual's spouse) is an active participant in an employer-sponsored retirement plan, the $2,000 deduction limit is phased out for taxpayers with modified adjusted gross income (MAGI) over certain levels for the taxable year.

The MAGI phaseout limits for taxpayers who are active participants in employer-sponsored plans are:

Single Taxpayers Taxable Years	*Phaseout Range*
2001	$33,000–$43,000
2002	$34,000–$44,000
2003	$40,000–$50,000
2004	$45,000–$55,000
2005 and thereafter	$50,000–$60,000

Joint Returns Taxable Years	Phaseout Range
2001	$53,000–$63,000
2002	$54,000–$64,000
2003	$60,000–$70,000
2004	$65,000–$75,000
2005	$70,000–$80,000
2006	$75,000–$85,000
2007 and thereafter	$80,000–$100,000

The MAGI phaseout range for married taxpayers filing a separate return is $0 to $10,000.

If the individual is not an active participant in an employer-sponsored retirement plan but the individual's spouse is, the $2,000 deduction limit is phased out for taxpayers with MAGI between $150,000 and $160,000.

If an individual cannot or does not make deductible contributions to an IRA or contributions to a Roth IRA, the individual may make nondeductible contributions to a traditional IRA. Amounts held in a traditional IRA are includable in income when withdrawn (except to the extent the withdrawal is a return of nondeductible contributions).

Includable amounts withdrawn prior to attainment of age $59\frac{1}{2}$ are subject to an additional 10 percent early withdrawal tax, unless the withdrawal is due to death or disability, is made in the form of certain periodic payments, is used to pay medical expenses in excess of 7.5 percent of AGI, is used to purchase health insurance of an unemployed individual, is used for education expenses, or is used for first-time home buyer expenses of up to $10,000.

ROTH IRAs. Individuals with MAGI below certain levels may make nondeductible contributions to Roth IRAs. The maximum annual contribution that may be made to a Roth IRA is the lesser of $2,000 or the individual's compensation for the year. The contribution limit is reduced to the extent an individual makes contributions to any other IRA for the same taxable year. As under the rules relating to IRAs generally, a contribution of up to $2,000 for each spouse may be made to a Roth IRA provided the combined compensation of the spouses is at least equal to the contributed amount. The maximum annual contribution that can be made to a Roth IRA is phased out for single individuals with modified adjusted gross income (MAGI) between $95,000 and $110,000 and for joint filers with MAGI between $150,000 and $160,000.

Taxpayers with MAGI of $100,000 or less generally may convert a traditional IRA into a Roth IRA. The amount converted is includable in income as if a withdrawal had been made, except that the 10 percent early withdrawal tax does not apply and, if the conversion occurred in 1998, the income inclusion may be spread ratably over four years. Married taxpayers who file separate returns cannot convert a traditional IRA into a Roth IRA.

Amounts held in a Roth IRA that are withdrawn as a qualified distribution are not includable in income or subject to the additional 10 percent tax on early withdrawals. A qualified distribution is a distribution that (1) is made after the five-taxable-year period beginning with the first taxable year for which the individual made a contribution to a Roth IRA, and (2) is made after attainment of age $59\frac{1}{2}$, on account of death or disability, or is made for first-time home buyer expenses of up to $10,000.

Distributions from a Roth IRA that are not qualified distributions are includable in income to the extent attributable to earnings, and subject to the 10 percent early withdrawal tax (unless an exception applies).

> **TIP**
>
> Early distribution of converted amounts may also accelerate income inclusion of converted amounts that are taxable under the four-year rule applicable to 1998 conversions.

The same exceptions to the early withdrawal tax that apply to IRAs apply to Roth IRAs.

New Law

INCREASE IN ANNUAL CONTRIBUTION LIMITS.   After 2001, the maximum annual dollar contribution limit for both traditional and Roth IRA contributions is increased as follows:

Year	Contribution Limit
2002–2004	$3,000
2005–2007	$4,000
2008	$5,000

After 2008, the $5,000 limit is adjusted annually for inflation in $500 increments.

ADDITIONAL CATCH-UP CONTRIBUTIONS.   After 2001, individuals who have attained age 50 may make additional catch-up IRA contributions. The otherwise maximum contribution limit (before application of the MAGI phaseout limits) for an individual who has attained age 50 before the end of the tax year is increased by $500 for 2002 through 2005, and $1,000 for 2006 and thereafter. The new catch-up maximums can be illustrated as follows:

Year	Contribution Limit (Including Catch-up)
2002–2004	$3,000 + $ 500 = $3,500
2005	$4,000 + $ 500 = $4,500
2006–2007	$4,000 + $1,000 = $5,000
2008 and thereafter	$5,000 + $1,000 = $6,000

Example

John Jones reaches age 50 during 2002. He has been contributing $2,000 to a Roth IRA annually since 1998. For 2002, John may contribute up to $3,500 to a Roth IRA, assuming the contribution limit does not have to be reduced because his modified AGI is in the $95,000 to $110,000 phaseout range for unmarried taxpayers.

As baby boomers edge closer to retirement, Congress is concerned about saving rates and the ability of individuals to establish sufficient retirement savings for themselves. Increased contribution limits and so-called catch-up provisions address these concerns. The catch-up provisions increase the contribution limit for older workers, allowing individuals who had to leave the workplace for a period of time to catch up to those who remained in the workforce. There is no requirement, however, that an individual had to have been absent from the workforce in order to access the catch-up contribution rates.

DEEMED IRAs UNDER EMPLOYER PLANS. After 2002, if an eligible retirement plan permits employees to make voluntary employee contributions to a separate account or annuity that (1) is established under the plan and (2) meets the requirements applicable to either traditional IRAs or Roth IRAs, then the separate account or annuity is deemed a traditional IRA or a Roth IRA, as applicable, for all purposes of the Internal Revenue Code.

> **TIP**
>
> Deemed IRAs allow employers to set up IRAs or Roth IRAs for their employees.

The IRA contribution limit applies to deemed IRAs. Since the limit is an overall limit, any contributions to traditional, Roth, and deemed IRAs must be taken into account. The reporting requirements applicable to IRAs apply to the deemed IRA.

The deemed IRA is not subject to the Code rules pertaining to the eligible retirement plans, but is subject to the exclusive benefit and Employee Retirement Income Security Act (ERISA) fiduciary rules. Thus, the deemed IRA is not subject to ERISA reporting and disclosure, participation, vesting, funding, and enforcement requirements generally applicable to qualified plans.

Qualified Plan Contributions and Benefits

Increase in Benefit and Contribution Limits

There are two categories of pension plans that are dealt with in this provision: defined contribution plans such as the 401(k), where the plan pays benefits based on contributions to individual accounts, and defined benefit plans, where the plan pays fixed benefits based on actuarial projections. The Tax Act of 2001 has increased both the contribution limits for defined contribution plans and the limits on annual benefits for defined benefit plans.

Pre-2001 Tax Act

Limits are imposed on contributions and benefits under qualified plans. The limits are based on the type of plan. Under a defined contribution plan, the qualification rules limit the annual additions to the plan with respect to each participant to the lesser of (1) 25 percent of compensation or (2) $35,000 (for 2001). The term "annual additions" is defined as the sum of employer contributions, employee contributions, and forfeitures with respect to an individual under all defined contribution plans of the same employer. The $35,000 limit is indexed for cost-of-living adjustments in $5,000 increments.

Under a defined benefit plan, the maximum annual benefit payable at retirement is generally the lesser of (1) 100 percent of average compensation or (2) $140,000 (for 2001). The dollar limit is adjusted for cost-of-living increases in $5,000 increments.

The dollar limit on annual benefits is reduced if benefits under the plan begin before the Social Security retirement age (currently age 65) and increased if benefits begin after Social Security retirement age.

New Law

For 2002, the $35,000 limit on annual additions to a defined contribution plan is increased to $40,000. This amount is indexed for inflation in increments of $1,000. Note that the 25 percent of compensation limitation no longer applies.

Also for 2002, the $140,000 annual benefit limit under a defined benefit plan is increased to $160,000. The dollar limit is now reduced for benefits beginning before age 62 (instead of 65 as previously) and still is increased for benefits beginning after age 65.

Compensation Limit

The amount of a participant's contributions to qualified plans is based on the contributor's compensation. Contribution limits are often placed on high earners in an attempt to limit their participation.

Pre-2001 Tax Act

The annual compensation of each participant that may be taken into account for purposes of determining contributions and benefits under a plan is limited to $170,000 (for 2001). This limit is indexed for cost-of-living adjustments and increases in $10,000 increments.

New Law

Beginning in 2002, the limit on compensation that may be taken into account under a plan is increased to $200,000. This amount will be indexed for cost-of-living adjustments and increased in $5,000 increments.

Elective Deferral Limitations

An elective deferral is simply a contribution made to a retirement plan by an employer as requested through an agreement with the employee. For example, an employee may request that an employer contribute $500 of the employee's salary to a 401(k) plan each month. This is an elective deferral. The term "deferral" is employed because taxes are deferred, as the amounts contributed are not included in gross income.

Pre-2001 Tax Act

The maximum annual amount of elective deferrals that an individual may make to a qualified cash or deferred arrangement (a 401(k) plan), a tax-sheltered annuity (a 403(b) annuity), or a salary-reduction simplified employee pension plan (SEP) is $10,500 (for 2001). The maximum annual amount of elective deferrals that an individual may make to a SIMPLE plan is $6,500 (for 2001). Both of these limits are indexed for inflation in $500 increments.

New Law

The dollar limit on annual elective deferrals under 401(k) plans, 403(b) annuities, and salary-reduction SEPs is increased. The new limits are:

Year	Limit
2002	$11,000
2003	$12,000
2004	$13,000
2005	$14,000
2006	$15,000

After 2006, the limits will be indexed for inflation in $500 increments.

The maximum annual elective deferrals that may be made to a SIMPLE plan is increased. The new limits are as follows:

Year	Limit
2002	$ 7,000
2003	$ 8,000
2004	$ 9,000
2005	$10,000

For years beginning after 2005, the $10,000 dollar limit is indexed for inflation in $500 increments.

Option to Treat Elective Deferrals as Roth Contributions

Beginning in 2005, participants in a qualified cash or deferred arrangement such as a 401(k) or 403(b) can elect to have their contributions treated as Roth IRA contributions. This will allow participants to receive distributions without including them in their taxable income.

Pre-2001 Tax Act

A qualified cash or deferred arrangement such as a 401(k) plan or a tax-sheltered annuity such as a 403(b) annuity may permit a participant to elect to have the employer make payments as contributions to the plan or to the participant directly in cash. Contributions made to the plan at the election of a participant are elective deferrals.

Individuals with adjusted gross income below certain levels generally may make nondeductible contributions to a Roth IRA and may convert a deductible or nondeductible IRA into a Roth IRA. Amounts held in a Roth IRA that are withdrawn as a qualified distribution are neither includable in income nor subject to the additional 10 percent tax on early withdrawals.

New Law

After 2005, a 401(k) plan or a 403(b) annuity may include a qualified Roth contribution program that permits a participant to elect to have all or a portion of the participant's elective deferrals under the plan treated as Roth contributions. Roth contributions are elective deferrals that the participant designates as not excludable from the participant's gross income. In this manner, a plan participant may elect to trade a current deferral of income for a future deferral of income.

Example

Jim participates in his company's 401(k) plan. In 2006, he decides to have one-half of his contributions treated as Roth contributions. Each month, Jim contributes $500 to his 401(k). Under his new allocation scheme, he will pay income tax on $250 of his monthly $500 contribution (i.e., the Roth portion). When the money is removed from his 401(k), all Roth contributions and corresponding earnings gains will be tax-free if they meet qualified distribution tests similar to those for Roth IRAs. A five-year waiting period will apply and the employee will have to be at least $59\frac{1}{2}$ years of age or disabled for the distributions from the designated Roth account to be tax-free. Distributions from the non-Roth portion of the 401(k) plan will be taxable.

Example

Jim participates in his company's 401(k) plan. In 2006 he is eligible to contribute $15,000 to the plan. If Jim elects to have $12,000 contributed to his 401(k) as pre-tax contributions, he can only designate $3,000 to be treated as a Roth contribution.

> The Conference Report noted that the IRS should provide ordering rules regarding the return of excess contributions under the special nondiscrimination rules in the event that a participant makes both regular elective deferrals and Roth contributions. The rules should generally permit a plan to allow participants to designate which contributions are returned first or permit the plan to specify which contributions are returned first. The Secretary should also provide ordering rules to determine the extent to which a distribution consists of excess Roth contributions.

The annual dollar limitation on elective deferrals includes amounts designated as Roth contributions.

Nonrefundable Credit to Certain Individuals for Elective Deferrals and IRA Contributions

Participation in private retirement plans such as the traditional IRA and Roth IRA has been rather low—especially in the case of lower- and middle-class taxpayers. In order to increase participation, the 2001 Tax Act has increased the benefits of participation in these plans for a limited time.

Pre-2001 Tax Act

Favorable tax treatment in the form of an exclusion or deduction is provided for contributions to employer-sponsored retirement plans and individual retirement accounts (IRAs). However, there is no tax credit for retirement plan contributions.

New Law

Beginning in 2002, a temporary, nonrefundable tax credit will be available for contributions made by eligible taxpayers to a qualified plan.

> **TIP**
>
> The credit is available in tax years beginning after 2001 and before 2007.

The maximum annual contribution eligible for the credit is $2,000. The amount of the credit available to the taxpayer depends on the taxpayer's modified adjusted gross income (MAGI). Only joint filers with MAGI of $50,000 or less, heads of household with $37,500 or less, and other filers with $25,000 or less are eligible for the credit. The MAGI limits applicable to single taxpayers also apply to married taxpayers filing separate returns. The credit is in addition to any deduction or exclusion that would otherwise apply with respect to the contribution and is available with respect to elective contributions to a 401(k) plan, 403(b) annuity, 457 plan, SIMPLE, SEP, or traditional or Roth IRA, and voluntary after-tax employee contributions to a qualified retirement plan.

The credit rates based on MAGI are as follows:

Joint Filers	Heads of Household	All Other Filers	Credit Rate
$0–$30,000	$0–$22,500	$0–$15,000	50%
$30,000–$32,500	$22,500–$24,375	$15,000–$16,250	20%
$32,500–$50,000	$24,375–$37,500	$16,250–$25,000	10%
Over $50,000	Over $37,500	Over $25,000	0%

Example

Jim and Mary are married and report an adjusted gross income (AGI) of $28,000 on their joint return. They both intend to contribute $600 to their IRAs in 2002. As would be the case under prior law, Jim and Mary will be able to deduct the $1,200 from their gross income for the year. But, as a result of the new law, they will also be able to claim a credit of $600 (50 percent credit rate for contributions of $1,200).

Contributions eligible for the credit are reduced by the amount of any taxable distributions received during the taxable year for which the credit is claimed and the two prior years. It is also reduced by any amounts received during the period after the end of the tax year and before the due date for filing the taxpayer's return for the year (generally between December 31 and April 15).

TIP

In the case of a distribution from a Roth IRA, the rule applies to any distributions, whether or not taxable.

The credit offsets alternative minimum tax liability as well as regular tax liability and is available to individuals who are 18 or over, other than individuals who are full-time students or a person who may be claimed as a dependent on another taxpayer's return.

The credit applies only for years 2002 through 2006.

Additional Deferrals for Employees Age 50 or Older

This provision appears in the section of the Act entitled "Enhancing Fairness for Women" and was designed to assist women who may have interrupted their employment to raise a family accumulate sufficient retirement savings. However, the increased limit on elective deferrals is not limited to women, and it applies regardless of prior employment history or level of contributions.

ADDITIONAL SALARY REDUCTION CATCH-UP CONTRIBUTIONS

Pre-2001 Tax Act

Under certain salary reduction arrangements, an employee may elect to have the employer make payments as contributions to a plan on behalf of the employee, such as a 401(k) plan. Contributions made at the election of the employee are called elective deferrals. These elective deferrals are limited as described earlier.

New Law

After 2001, the limits on elective deferrals for a 401(k) plan, 403(b) annuity, SEP, or SIMPLE, or deferrals under a 457 plan are increased for individuals who have attained age 50 by the end of the year.

The increases for 401(k), 403(b) annuity, SEP, or 457 plans are:

Year	Increase
2002	$1,000
2003	$2,000
2004	$3,000
2005	$4,000
2006 and thereafter	$5,000

For SIMPLE plans:

Year	Increase
2002	$ 500
2003	$1,000
2004	$1,500
2005	$2,000
2006 and thereafter	$2,500

The $5,000 and $2,500 amounts are adjusted for inflation in $500 increments in 2007 and thereafter.

The catch-up contribution provision does not apply to after-tax employee contributions.

Additional contributions may be made by an individual who has attained age 50 before the end of the plan year and with respect to whom no other elective deferrals may otherwise be made to the plan for the year because of the application of any limitation of the Code (e.g., the annual limit on elective deferrals) or of the plan. The additional amount of elective contributions that may be made by an eligible individual participating in such a plan is the lesser of (1) the applicable dollar amount or (2) the participant's compensation for the year reduced by any other elective deferrals of the participant for the year.

TIP

In the case of a 457 plan, this catch-up rule does not apply during the participant's last three years before retirement (in those years, the regularly applicable dollar limit is doubled).

Example 1

In 2006 Kelly, who is over 50, is a participant in a 401(k) plan. Kelly's compensation is $30,000. The maximum annual deferral limit (without regard to this provision) is $15,000. Under the terms of the plan, the maximum permitted deferral is 10 percent of compensation or, in Kelly's case, $3,000. Under this provision, Kelly can contribute up to $8,000 for the year ($3,000 under the normal operation of the plan and an additional $5,000 catch-up contribution).

Example 2

In 2006 Joan is a highly compensated employee who is over 50 and who participates in a 401(k) plan sponsored by her employer. The maximum annual deferral limit (without regard to this provision) is $15,000. After application of the special nondiscrimination rules applicable to 401(k) plans, the maximum elective deferral that Joan may make for the year is $8,000. Under this provision, Joan is able to make additional catch-up salary reduction contributions of $5,000.

PENSION AND INDIVIDUAL RETIREMENT ARRANGEMENT RELIEF

The following examples illustrate the application of the catch-up provision when fully phased in.

Catch-up contributions are not subject to any other contribution limits and are not taken into account in applying other contribution limits. In addition, such contributions are not subject to nondiscrimination rules. However, a plan fails to meet nondiscrimination requirements unless the plan allows all eligible individuals participating in the plan to make the same election with respect to catch-up contributions. Employer matching contributions may be made with respect to catch-up contributions, but are subject to normal rules.

Faster Vesting of Employer Matching Contributions

This is another provision that appears under the section "Enhancing Fairness for Women." It shortens the time frame in which an employee vests in employer matching contributions. Faster vesting of matching contributions is intended to encourage plan participation by workers who will not remain with one employer for many years. Women, in particular, may have fewer years with the same employer due to family obligations.

Pre-2001 Tax Act

A plan is not a qualified plan unless a participant's employer-provided benefit vests at least as rapidly as under one of two alternative minimum vesting schedules. A plan satisfies the first schedule if a participant acquires a nonforfeitable right to 100 percent of the participant's accrued benefit derived from employer contributions upon the completion of five years of service. A plan satisfies the second schedule if a participant has a nonforfeitable right to at least 20 percent of the participant's accrued benefit derived from employer contributions after three years of service, 40 percent after four years of service, 60 percent after five years of service, 80 percent after six years of service, and 100 percent after seven years of service.

New Law

After 2001, faster vesting schedules apply to employer matching contributions. Employer matching contributions are required to vest at least as rapidly as under one of the following two alternative minimum vesting schedules. A plan satisfies the first schedule if a participant acquires a nonforfeitable right to 100 percent of employer matching contributions upon the completion of three years of service. A plan satisfies the second schedule if a participant has a nonforfeitable right to 20 percent of employer matching contributions for each year of service beginning

A delayed effective date applies for plans maintained pursuant to a collective bargaining agreement. The faster vesting schedule does not apply to any employee until the employee has an hour of service after 2001. In applying the new vesting schedule, service before the effective date is taken into account.

with the participant's second year of service and ending with 100 percent after six years of service.

Modifications to Minimum Distribution Rules

The minimum distribution rules were significantly modified and simplified by proposed regulations issued this year, but the life expectancy tables have not been amended. Since life expectancy has increased, the update of the tables will have the effect of increasing payout periods and decreasing minimum distributions required.

Pre-2001 Tax Act

Minimum distribution rules apply to IRAs, qualified plans, 403(b) annuities, and 457 plans. In general, under these rules, distribution of minimum benefits must begin no later than the required beginning date. For distributions prior to the death of the plan participant, the minimum distribution rules are generally satisfied if either (1) the participant's entire interest in the plan is distributed by the required beginning date, or (2) the participant's interest in the plan is to be distributed (in accordance with regulations), beginning not later than the required beginning date, over a permissible period. The permissible periods are (1) the life of the participant, (2) the lives of the participant and a designated beneficiary, (3) the life expectancy of the participant, or (4) the joint life and last survivor expectancy of the participant and a designated beneficiary.

New Law

The Treasury must revise the life expectancy tables under the applicable regulations to reflect current life expectancy, effective June 7, 2001.

457 Plans

Named after the tax code section that gave rise to these plans, 457 plans allow state and local governments and tax-exempt organizations to offer deferred compensation plans to their employees. The amount of compensation that a participant may defer is limited. The Tax Act of 2001 increases the limitation on these contributions.

Pre-2001 Tax Act

The maximum annual deferral under a deferred compensation plan of a state or local government or a tax-exempt organization to a 457 plan is the lesser of (1) $8,500 (for 2001) or (2) $33\frac{1}{3}$ percent of an employee's compensation. The $8,500 amount is increased for inflation in $500 increments.

Under a special catch-up rule, the 457 plan may provide that, for one or more of the participant's last three years before normal retirement age is reached, the otherwise applicable limit is increased to the lesser of (1) $15,000 or (2) $8,500 (for 2001) plus the amount by which deferrals in preceding years fell short of the applicable limit.

Example

Jim is 62 in 2001—three years before normal retirement age of 65 will be reached. This year, he is able to contribute the full $8,500 to his 457 plan. Jim fell short of the maximum contribution by $6,000 in 1990, $2,000 in 1997, and $1,500 in 1998 (for a total underutilization of $9,500). This year, Jim can catch up by contributing his $8,500 plus $6,500 of his $9,500 underutilization (he is limited by the $15,000 rule). In the next year, Jim will be able to contribute the remaining $3,000.

New Law

The contribution limit will be $11,000 in 2002, and is increased in $1,000 annual increments thereafter until the limit reaches $15,000 in 2006:

Tax Year	Limit Amount
2002	$11,000
2003	$12,000
2004	$13,000
2005	$14,000
2006	$15,000

Beginning in 2007, the limit will be indexed for inflation in $500 increments. (Note that the 33⅓ percent limitation no longer applies.)

The limitation on the catch-up provision has also been

Example

Assume the same facts as in the preceding example, but that Jim is 62 in year 2002. He will be able to contribute all of the $9,500 deferral underutilization because the limitation for catching up now is twice the normal limitation or $22,000.

raised. For tax years beginning after 2001, the limit is twice the otherwise applicable dollar limit (or $22,000 in 2002).

TAX TREATMENT OF THE DIVISION OF 457 PLAN BENEFITS UPON DIVORCE
Prior to the 2001 Tax Act, distributions from 457 plans that were distributed to the spouse (or former spouse) of the participant by reason of a qualified domestic relations order (QDRO) were not taxable to the spouse. The 2001 Tax Act changes this provision as well as another dealing with distributions to those other than the participant in a 457 plan.

Pre-2001 Tax Act

Benefits provided under a qualified retirement plan for a participant may not be assigned or alienated to creditors of the participant, except in very limited circumstances. One exception to the prohibition on assignment or alienation rule is a qualified domestic relations order (QDRO). A

QDRO is a domestic relations order that creates or recognizes a right of an alternate payee to any plan benefit payable with respect to a participant, and that meets certain procedural requirements.

Amounts distributed from a plan generally are taxable to the participant in the year of distribution. However, if amounts are distributed to the spouse (or former spouse) of the participant by reason of a QDRO, the benefits are taxable to the spouse (or former spouse). Amounts distributed pursuant to a QDRO to an alternate payee other than the spouse (or former spouse) are taxable to the plan participant. These QDRO rules do not apply to 457 plans.

New Law

For distributions and payments after 2001, the taxation rules for qualified plan distributions pursuant to a QDRO apply to distributions made pursuant to a domestic relations order from a 457 plan. In addition, a 457 plan does not violate the restrictions on distributions from such plans due to payments to an alternate payee under a QDRO.

MINIMUM DISTRIBUTION AND INCLUSION REQUIREMENTS FOR 457 PLANS

Participants in 457 plans were taxed on deferred amounts distributions when paid or when made *available*. The Tax Act of 2001 makes deferrals taxable only when paid.

Pre-2001 Tax Act

Amounts deferred under a 457 plan are generally includable in income when paid or made available. Amounts deferred under a plan of deferred compensation of a state or local government or tax-exempt employer that does not meet the requirements of Section 457 are includable in income when the amounts are not subject to a substantial risk of forfeiture, regardless of whether the amounts have been paid or made available.

TIP

This rule of inclusion does not apply to amounts deferred under a tax-qualified retirement plan or similar plans.

A 457 plan is subject to the minimum distribution rules, as well as additional minimum distribution rules.

New Law

After 2001, amounts deferred under a 457 plan of a state or local government are includable in income only when paid. The special minimum distribution rules applicable to 457 plans are repealed. Effective for distributions after 2001, such plans are subject to the minimum distribution rules applicable to qualified plans.

TIP

This provision applies only to a 457 plan of a state or local government; 457 plans of tax-exempt employers are subject to the prior-law rules.

Provisions Relating to Hardship Withdrawals

Participants in qualified plans may not withdraw money from their plans unless one or more specific events occurs. One of these events is a hardship withdrawal. There are "safe harbor" rules that deem a distribution necessary for a hardship if the rules are met. Included in the safe harbor rules is the provision that the participant may not make a withdrawal for hardship and then contribute to the plan for at least 12 months after receiving the distribution. The Tax Act of 2001 diminishes this period.

Pre-2001 Tax Act

Elective deferrals under a 401(k) plan may not be distributable prior to the occurrence of one or more specified events. One event upon which distribution is permitted is the financial hardship of the employee. Treasury regulations provide that a distribution is made on account of hardship only if the distribution is made on account of an immediate and heavy financial need of the employee and is necessary to satisfy the heavy need. A similar hardship rule applies to 403(b) plans.

The regulations provide a safe harbor under which a distribution may be deemed necessary to satisfy an immediate and heavy financial need. One requirement of this safe harbor is that the employee be prohibited from making elective contributions and employee contributions to the plan and all other plans maintained by the employer for at least 12 months after receipt of the hardship distribution.

Hardship withdrawals of elective deferrals from a 401(k) plan or 403(b) plan are not eligible rollover distributions. Other types of hardship distributions (e.g., employer matching contributions distributed on account of hardship) are eligible rollover distributions.

New Law

The IRS has been directed to revise the applicable regulations to reduce from 12 months to 6 months the period during which an employee must be prohibited from making elective contributions and employee contributions in order for a distribution to be deemed necessary to satisfy an immediate and heavy financial need. The revised regulations are to be effective for years beginning after 2001.

TIP

This provision is intended to clarify that all assets distributed as a hardship withdrawal, including assets attributable to employee elective deferrals and those attributable to employer matching or nonelective contributions, are ineligible for rollover.

The rationale for the prohibition against employee contributions for 12 months after a hardship event was that in the case of an actual financial hardship situation, an employee should not in fact have funds to contribute to a qualified plan. However, the length of the prohibition was deemed punitive in that it may impose additional financial hardship by preventing the tax-free accumulation of funds for retirement.

Any distribution made upon hardship of an employee is not an eligible rollover distribution. Thus, such distributions may not be rolled over, and are subject to the withholding rules applicable to distributions that are not eligible rollover distributions.

Pension Coverage for Domestic and Similar Workers

The 2001 Tax Act removes the 10 percent excise tax that applies to nondeductible contributions to SIMPLE plans on behalf of domestic employees.

Pre-2001 Tax Act

Within limits, employers may make deductible contributions to qualified retirement plans for employees. Subject to certain exceptions, a 10 percent excise tax applies to nondeductible contributions to such plans. Employers of household workers may establish a pension plan for their employees. Contributions to such plans are not deductible because they are not made in connection with a trade or business of the employer.

New Law

After 2001, the 10 percent excise tax on nondeductible contributions does not apply to contributions to a SIMPLE plan

or a SIMPLE IRA that are nondeductible solely because the
contributions are not a trade or
business expense under Section
162 because they are not made
in connection with a trade or
business of the employer. Contributions for the employer or
the employer's family members
do not qualify.

> **TIP**
>
> As a result of the new provision, employers of household workers may contribute to SIMPLE plans without imposition of the excise tax. The contributions still may not be deducted.

The Conference Report warned that the provision should
apply only if the employer has and continues to pay all employment taxes.

Increasing Portability for Participants

Rollovers of Retirement Plan and IRA Distributions

The new tax law increases the rollover options for retirement plan participants.

Pre-2001 Tax Act

The rollover of funds is generally allowed from one qualified plan to another, depending on the type of plan involved.

An "eligible rollover distribution" from a tax-qualified
employer-sponsored retirement plan may be rolled over
tax-free to a traditional individual retirement account (IRA)
or another qualified plan.

Eligible rollover distributions from a 403(b) tax-sheltered

TIP

Qualified plans are not required to accept rollovers.

annuity may be rolled over into a traditional IRA or another 403(b) annuity. Distributions from a 403(b) annuity cannot be rolled over into a tax-qualified plan.

Distributions from a traditional IRA, other than minimum required distributions, can be rolled over into another IRA. Generally, distributions from an IRA cannot be rolled over into a qualified plan or 403(b) annuity.

Distributions from a 457 plan cannot be rolled over to another 457 plan, a qualified plan, a section 403(b) annuity, or an IRA.

A surviving spouse who receives an eligible rollover distribution may roll over the distribution into an IRA, but not a qualified plan or 403(b) annuity.

New Law

After 2001, eligible rollover distributions from qualified retirement plans, 403(b) annuities, and governmental 457 plans generally may be rolled over to any of such plans or arrangements. Similarly, distributions from an IRA generally may be rolled over into a qualified plan, 403(b) annuity, or governmental 457 plan. The direct rollover and withholding rules are extended to distributions from a governmental 457 plan, and such plans are required to provide the written notification regarding eligible rollover distributions.

Employee after-tax contributions may be rolled over into another qualified plan or a traditional IRA. In the case of a rollover from a qualified plan to another qualified plan, the rollover is permitted to be accomplished only through a direct rollover. In addition, a qualified plan is not permitted to accept rollovers of after-tax contributions unless the plan provides separate accounting for such contributions (and

> **TIP**
>
> Hardship distributions from 457 plans are not considered eligible rollover distributions. Nongovernmental 457 plans are excluded from these liberalized rollover rules.

earnings thereon). After-tax nondeductible contributions are not permitted to be rolled over from an IRA into a qualified plan, tax-sheltered annuity, or 457 plan.

Surviving spouses may roll over distributions to a qualified plan, 403(b) annuity, or 457 plan in which the surviving spouse participates.

Example

Ken predeceases his spouse Jane, and the balance of his 401(k) plan is payable to Jane. Before 2002, Jane could roll over the amount only into an IRA (but Jane was allowed to treat the IRA as her own). After 2001, Jane may roll over the balance to her employer's qualified plan in which she participates, a 403(b) annuity, or a 457 plan.

Waiver of 60-Day Rule

Generally, distributions from an IRA or qualified plan may be rolled over tax-free if the rollover is made within 60 days. The Tax Act of 2001 gives the IRS the authority to waive this rule in some circumstances.

Under prior law, the strict application of the 60-day rule resulted in inequities when taxpayers were denied favorable rollover treatment due to errors beyond their control, such as when a financial institution failed to properly follow the taxpayer's instructions as to the deposit of funds.

Pre-2001 Tax Act

Amounts received from an IRA or qualified plan may be rolled over tax-free if the rollover is made within 60 days of the date of the distribution. The IRS does not have the authority to waive the 60-day requirement, except during military service in a combat zone or by reason of a presidentially declared disaster.

New Law

For distributions after 2001, the IRS may waive the 60-day rollover period if the failure to waive such requirement would be against equity or good conscience, including cases of casualty, disaster, or other events beyond the reasonable control of the individual subject to such requirement. For example, the Secretary may issue guidance that includes objective standards for a waiver of the 60-day rollover period, such as waiving the rule for a period during which the participant has received payment in the form of a check but has not cashed the check, for errors committed by a financial institution, or in cases of inability to complete a rollover due to death, disability, hospitalization, incarceration, restrictions imposed by a foreign country, or postal error.

Automatic Rollovers of Certain Mandatory Distributions

The Tax Act of 2001 requires that the default option for some involuntary distributions is to roll over the amounts to a designated IRA.

Pre-2001 Tax Act

Generally, a participant may roll over an involuntary distribution (see the discussion of cash-out provisions, p. 173) from a qualified plan to an IRA or to another qualified plan. Before making a distribution that is eligible for rollover, a plan administrator must provide the participant with a written explanation of the ability to have the distribution rolled over directly to an IRA or another qualified plan, and the related tax consequences.

New Law

A direct rollover is the default option for involuntary distributions that exceed $1,000 and that are eligible rollover distributions from qualified retirement plans. The distribution must be rolled over automatically to a designated IRA, unless the participant affirmatively elects to have the distribution transferred to a different IRA or a qualified plan or to receive it directly.

EFFECTIVE DATE. The provision applies to distributions that occur after the Department of Labor has adopted final regulations implementing the provision, which must be adopted by June 7, 2004.

Explanation of Tax Consequences for Recipients of Rollover Distributions

This provision increases the amount of information that a plan administrator must provide to recipients of distributions. The newly required information will help increase participants' understanding of the different tax consequences surrounding tax-favored retirement plans. It is hoped that this will help participants avoid rolling their funds into plans that do not offer the same advantages.

Pre-2001 Tax Act

A plan administrator is required to provide written notice of the options available to the recipient of an eligible rollover distribution. The notice must describe: the rules under which the recipient can transfer the distribution directly into another eligible retirement plan; the rules that require withholding if the distribution is not transferred to another eligible retirement plan; the rule that states that the distribution may be rolled over into an eligible plan within 60 days; and any other provisions relating to the distribution.

New Law

Starting in 2002, the plan administrator must include in the notice (apart from the information just described) an explanation of how the distributions from the plan to which the distribution is being rolled over may not have the same tax consequences as the plan from which the distribution came.

Treatment of Forms of Distribution

Requirements that do not allow an amendment to a qualified plan that decreases the accrued benefit of a plan participant have been eased.

The purpose of this easing is to permit the elimination of certain optional forms of benefits after merger that have no more than a *de minimis* effect on any participant, even if they create disproportionate burdens and complexities for a plan and its participants.

Pre-2001 Tax Act

An amendment of a qualified retirement plan may not decrease the accrued benefit of a plan participant. An amendment is treated as reducing an accrued benefit if, with

TIP

These rules are known as the anticutback rules.

respect to benefits accrued before the amendment is adopted, the amendment has the effect of either (1) eliminating or reducing an early retirement benefit or a retirement-type subsidy, or (2) except as provided by Treasury regulations, eliminating an optional form of benefit.

Under recently issued regulations, this prohibition against the elimination of an optional form of benefit does not apply in the case of (1) a defined contribution plan that offers a lump sum at the same time as the form being eliminated if the participant receives at least 90 days' advance notice of the elimination, or (2) a voluntary transfer between defined contribution plans, subject to the requirements that a transfer from a money purchase pension plan, an employee stock ownership plan (ESOP), or a 401(k) plan must be to a plan of the same type and that the transfer be made in connection with certain corporate mergers, acquisitions, or similar transactions or changes in employment status.

New Law

After 2001, a defined contribution plan to which benefits are transferred will not be treated as reducing a participant's or beneficiary's accrued benefit even though it does not provide all of the forms of distribution previously available under the transferor plan if (1) the plan receives from another defined contribution plan a direct transfer of the participant's or beneficiary's benefit accrued under the transferor plan, or the plan results from a merger or other transaction that has the effect of a direct transfer (including consolidations of benefits attributable to different employers within a multiple-employer plan), (2) the terms of both the transferor plan and the transferee plan authorize the transfer, (3) the transfer occurs pursuant to a voluntary election by the participant or beneficiary that is made after the participant or beneficiary received a notice describing the consequences of making the election, and (4) the transferee plan allows the participant or beneficiary to receive distribution of his or her benefit under the transferee plan in the form of a single-sum distribution.

TIP

The rules relating to survivor annuities under Section 417 are not modified. Thus, a plan that is a transferee of a plan subject to the joint and survivor rules is also subject to those rules.

Except to the extent provided by regulations, a defined contribution plan is not treated as reducing a participant's

---

The IRS is directed to provide by regulations that the prohibitions against eliminating or reducing an early retirement benefit, a retirement-type subsidy, or an optional form of benefit do not apply to plan amendments that eliminate or reduce early retirement benefits, retirement-type subsidies, and optional forms of benefit that create significant burdens and complexities for a plan and its participants, but only if such an amendment does not adversely affect the rights of any participant in more than a *de minimis* manner.

Example

Employer A acquires Employer B and merges B's defined benefit plan into A's defined benefit plan. The defined benefit plan maintained by B before the merger provides an early retirement subsidy for individuals age 55 with a specified number of years of service. Linda and Mark were employees of B who transfer to A in connection with the merger. Linda is 25 years old and has compensation of $40,000. The present value of Linda's early retirement subsidy under B's plan is $75. Mark is 50 years old and also has compensation of $40,000. The present value of Mark's early retirement subsidy under B's plan is $10,000.

A's plan has an early retirement subsidy for individuals who have attained age 50 with a specified number of years of service, but the subsidy is not the same as under B's plan. Under A's plan, the present value of Mark's early retirement subsidy is $9,850. Maintenance of both subsidies after the plan merger would create burdens for the plan and complexities for the plan and its participants.

Treasury regulations could permit Linda's early retirement subsidy under B's plan to be eliminated entirely (i.e., even if A's plan did not have an early retirement subsidy). Taking into account all relevant factors, including the value of the benefit, Linda's compensation, and the number of years until Linda would be eligible to receive the subsidy, the subsidy is *de minimis*. Treasury regulations could permit Mark's early retirement subsidy under B's plan to be eliminated and to be replaced by the subsidy under A's plan, because the difference in the subsidies is *de minimis*. However, A's subsidy could not be entirely eliminated.

accrued benefit if (1) a plan amendment eliminates a form of distribution previously available under the plan, (2) a single-sum distribution is available to the participant at the same time or times as the form of distribution eliminated by the amendment, and (3) the single-sum distribution is based on the same or greater portion of the participant's accrued benefit as the form of distribution eliminated by the amendment.

The provision does not affect the rules relating to involuntary cash-outs or survivor annuity requirements.

Business Owners and Plan Administration

Notice of Significant Reduction in Plan Benefit

Pre-2001 Tax Act

Section 204(h) of Title I of ERISA provides that a defined benefit pension plan or a money purchase pension plan may not be amended so as to provide for a significant reduction in the rate of future benefit accrual unless, after adoption of the plan amendment and not less than 15 days before the effective date of the plan amendment, the plan administrator provides a written notice (Section 204(h) notice), setting forth the plan amendment (or a summary of the amendment written in a manner calculated to be understood by the average plan participant) and its effective date. The plan administrator must provide the Section 204(h) notice to each plan participant, each alternate payee under an applicable qualified domestic relations order (QDRO), and each employee organization representing participants in the plan.

Treasury regulations provide, however, that a plan administrator need not provide the Section 204(h) notice to any participant or alternate payee whose rate of future benefit accrual is reasonably expected not to be reduced by the amendment, nor to an employee organization that does not represent a participant to whom the Section 204(h) notice must be provided. In addition, the regulations provide that the rate of future benefit accrual is determined without regard to optional forms of benefit, early retirement benefits, retirement-type subsidiaries, ancillary benefits, and certain other rights and features.

The Internal Revenue Code does not require any notice concerning a plan amendment that provides for a significant reduction in the rate of future benefit accrual.

New Law

Effective June 7, 2001, a requirement is added to the Internal Revenue Code that the plan administrator of a defined benefit pension plan or a money purchase pension plan furnish a written notice concerning a plan amendment that provides for a significant reduction in the rate of future benefit accrual, including any elimination or reduction of an early retirement benefit or retirement-type subsidy. A plan administrator that fails to comply with the notice requirement is subject to an excise tax equal to $100 per day per omitted participant and alternate payee.

Deduction Limits

Pre-2001 Tax Act

Employer contributions to qualified retirement plans are deductible subject to limits that depend on the kind of plan.

> **TIP**
> Nondeductible contributions are generally subject to a 10 percent excise tax.

For purposes of the deduction rules, compensation generally includes only taxable compensation, and thus does not include salary reduction amounts, such as elective deferrals under a section 401(k) plan or a 403(b) tax-sheltered annuity, elective contributions under a deferred compensation plan of a tax-exempt organization or a state or local government (457 plan), and salary reduction contributions under a Section 125 cafeteria plan. For purposes of the contribution limits under Section 415, compensation does include such salary reduction amounts.

New Law

Starting in 2002, the annual limitation on the amount of deductible contributions to a profit sharing or stock bonus plan is increased from 15 percent to 25 percent of compensation of the employees covered by the plan for the year. In addition, the definition of compensation for purposes of the

> **TIP**
> An increase in items included in compensation for purposes of the deduction rules may increase an employer's deduction limit and thereby enhance the desirability of maintaining qualified plans.

deduction rules includes salary reduction amounts treated as compensation under Section 415. Also, except to the extent provided in regulations, a money purchase pension plan is treated like a profit sharing or stock bonus plan for purposes of the deduction rules.

Plan Loans for S Corporation Shareholders, Partners, and Sole Proprietors

TIP

These transactions are known as prohibited transactions.

The Internal Revenue Code prohibits certain transactions between a qualified plan and people with a close relationship to the qualified plan. This is to stop such people from using that relationship to the detriment of plan participants and beneficiaries.

Pre-2001 Tax Act

Although there are exemptions to "prohibited transactions," these exemptions don't apply to an owner-employee. The term "owner-employee" includes:

- A sole proprietor.
- A partner who owns more than 10 percent of either the capital interest or the profits interest in a partnership.
- An employee or officer of an S corporation who owns more than 5 percent of the outstanding stock of the corporation.

New Law

After 2001, the prior-law restrictions on plan loans to owner-employees are eliminated. Starting in 2002, loans can be made to S corporation shareholders, partners in partnerships, and sole proprietors of unincorporated businesses under the same rules applicable to C corporation shareholders. The new rule may encourage owner-employees to establish qualified plans.

Modification of Top-Heavy Rules

IN GENERAL. Additional qualification requirements apply to plans that primarily benefit an employer's key employees (top-heavy plans). This is often the situation in small businesses where there are few employees, many of whom qualify as key employees.

These additional requirements provide (1) more rapid vesting for plan participants who are nonkey employees and (2) minimum nonintegrated employer contributions or benefits for plan participants who are nonkey employees.

DEFINITION OF TOP-HEAVY PLAN

Pre-2001 Tax Act

A plan is considered a top-heavy plan if more than 60 percent of the account balances or accrued benefits are for key employees. For each plan year, the determination of top-heavy status generally is made as of the last day of the preceding plan year (the determination date).

New Law

After 2001, 401(k) plans will not be considered top-heavy if they satisfy the 401(k) design-based nondiscrimination safe-harbor rules and meet the matching contributions safe harbor. As a result, a plan that satisfies the safe harbors not only will satisfy 401(k) nondiscrimination requirements, but will not be a top-heavy plan.

TIP

The effect of this provision is to increase the desirability of 401(k) plans for small businesses.

Matching or nonelective contributions may be taken into account in satisfying the minimum contribution requirements for top-heavy plans. The contributions may also be used to satisfy other qualified plan nondiscrimination rules.

DEFINITION OF KEY EMPLOYEE

The new tax law changes the rules for determining whether an employee is a key employee.

Pre-2001 Tax Act

A key employee is an employee who during the plan year or any of the four preceding years is (1) an officer earning over one-half of the defined benefit plan dollar limitation of Section 415 ($70,000 for 2001), (2) a 5 percent owner of the employer, (3) a 1 percent owner of the employer earning over $150,000, or (4) one of the 10 employees earning more than the defined contribution plan dollar limit ($35,000 for 2001) with the largest ownership interests in the employer. A family ownership attribution rule applies to the determination of 1 percent owner status, 5 percent owner status, and largest ownership interest. Under this attribution rule, an individual is treated as owning stock owned by the individual's spouse, children, grandchildren, or parents.

New Law

After 2001, an employee is a key employee if, during the prior year, the employee was (1) an officer with compensation in excess of $130,000 (adjusted for inflation in $5,000 increments), (2) a 5 percent owner, or (3) a 1 percent owner with compensation in excess of $150,000. The old law limits on the number of officers treated as key employees continue to apply, as do the family ownership attribution rules.

MINIMUM BENEFIT FOR NONKEY EMPLOYEES

Pre-2001 Tax Act

A minimum benefit generally must be provided to all non-key employees in a top-heavy plan. In general, a top-heavy defined benefit plan must provide a minimum benefit equal to the lesser of (1) 2 percent of compensation multiplied by the employee's years of service or (2) 20 percent of compensation. A top-heavy defined contribution plan must provide a minimum annual contribution equal to the lesser of (1) 3 percent of compensation or (2) the percentage of compensation at which contributions were made for key employees (including employee elective contributions made by key employees and employer matching contributions).

Only benefits derived from employer contributions (other than elective deferrals) to the plan are taken into account. Employer matching contributions may be used to satisfy the minimum contribution requirement, but, if so, the contributions are not treated as matching contributions for purposes of applying the special nondiscrimination requirements applicable to employee elective contributions and matching contributions under Code sections 401(k) and (m). Thus, such contributions would have to meet the general nondiscrimination rules.

New Law

After 2001, matching contributions are taken into account in determining whether the minimum benefit requirement has been satisfied. This provision overrides the Treasury regulations, which provide that if matching contributions are used to satisfy the minimum benefit requirement, then they are not treated as matching contributions for purposes of the Section 401(m) nondiscrimination rules.

In determining the minimum benefit required under a defined benefit plan, years of service do not include any year in which no key employee or former key employee benefits under the plan.

Elective Deferrals Not Taken into Account for Purposes of Deduction Limits

Pre-2001 Tax Act

Employer contributions to one or more qualified retirement plans are deductible subject to certain limits that depend on the kind of plan. Employee elective deferral contributions to a 401(k) plan and other salary reduction plans are treated as employer contributions and thus are subject to the generally applicable deduction limits.

Example

Ian elects to contribute 2 percent ($2,000) of his salary ($100,000) to his employer's 401(k) plan. The employer's deduction limit (15 percent of employees' compensation for years before 2002) for other contributions will be decreased by $2,000.

New Law

After 2001, elective deferral contributions are not subject to the deduction limits, and the application of a deduction limitation to any other employer contribution to a

TIP

This provision neutralizes the effect of elective contributions on the employer's deduction, thus making provisions for elective contributions more desirable for employers.

qualified retirement plan does not take into account elective deferral contributions. This rule applies to elective deferral contributions made to 401(k) plans, 403(b) plans, salary reduction SEPs, and SIMPLE plans.

Example

Ian elects to contribute 2 percent ($2,000) of his salary ($100,000) to his employer's 401(k) plan. The employer's deduction limit (increased from 15 percent to 25 percent of employees' compensation for years after 2001) will not be decreased by the amount of the elective deferral.

Repeal of Coordination Requirements for Deferred Compensation Plans of State and Local Governments and Tax-Exempt Organizations

Under the pre-2001 Tax Act law, limitations on contributions to 457 plans took into account contributions to other qualified plans such as the 401(k), 403(b), and SIMPLE plans. Thus, contributions to other plans effectively limited the amount that could be contributed to the 457 plan. The new tax law repeals this cumulative limitation.

Pre-2001 Tax Act

Compensation deferred under an eligible deferred compensation plan of a tax-exempt or state and local government employer (a 457 plan) is not includable in gross income until paid or made available. Generally, the maximum permitted annual deferral under such a plan is the lesser of (1) $8,500 (in 2001) or (2) $33\frac{1}{3}$ percent of compensation. The $8,500 limit is increased for inflation in $500 increments. Under a special catch-up rule, a 457 plan may provide that, for one or more of the participant's last three years before retirement, the otherwise applicable limit is increased to the lesser of (1) $15,000 or (2) the sum of the otherwise applicable limit for the year plus the amount by which the limit applicable in preceding years of participation exceeded the deferrals for that year.

The $8,500 limit applies to all deferrals under all 457 plans in which the individual participates. The limit is reduced by contributions to a 403(b) annuity, elective deferrals to a 401(k) plan, salary reduction contributions under a simplified employee pension plan (SEP), and contributions under a SIMPLE plan. Further, the amount deferred under a 457 plan is taken into account in applying a special catch-up rule for 403(b) annuities.

Example

Harry contributes $1,000 to a SEP. The limitation for his contribution to a 457 plan ($8,500) is reduced by $1,000 to $7,500.

New Law

The rules coordinating the 457 plan dollar limit with contributions under other types of plans is repealed, effective after 2001.

Example

In 2002, Harry contributes $1,000 to a SEP. The limitation for his contribution to a 457 plan is not reduced.

Elimination of IRS User Fees for Certain Determination Letter Requests Regarding Employer Plans

An employer may request a determination from the IRS verifying that its retirement plan meets the requirements for a qualified plan. This request usually requires a fee for processing. The new tax law eliminates this fee in certain circumstances.

Pre-2001 Tax Act

For a fee, an employer that maintains a retirement plan for the benefit of employees may request from the IRS a determination as to whether the form of the plan satisfies the requirements applicable to tax-qualified plans. The Secretary determines the user fee applicable for various types of requests, subject to statutory minimum requirements for average fees based on the category of the request. The user fee may range from $125 to $1,250, depending on the scope of the request and the type and format of the plan.

New Law

For determination letter requests made after 2001, a small employer (100 or fewer employees and at least one non–highly compensated employee who is participating in the plan) is not required to pay a user fee for a determination letter request with respect to the qualified status of a retirement plan that the employer maintains if the request is made before the later of (1) the last day of the fifth plan year of the plan or (2) the end of any applicable remedial amendment period with respect to the plan that begins before the end of the fifth plan year of the plan.

The provision applies only to requests by employers for determination letters concerning the qualified retirement plans they maintain. Therefore, a sponsor of a prototype plan is required to pay a user fee for a request for a notification letter, opinion letter, or similar ruling. A small employer that adopts a prototype plan, however, is not required to pay a user fee for a determination letter request with respect to the employer's plan. This provision is one of many that attempts to increase the appeal of qualified plans for small employers.

Small Business Tax Credit for New Retirement Plan Expenses

Pre-2001 Tax Act

The costs incurred by an employer related to the establishment and maintenance of a retirement plan (e.g., payroll system changes, investment vehicle setup fees, consulting fees) generally are deductible by the employer as ordinary and necessary expenses in carrying on a trade or business.

New Law

A nonrefundable income tax credit is provided for a portion of the administrative and retirement-education expenses for any small business that, after 2001, adopts a new qualified defined benefit or defined contribution plan such as a 401(k) plan, a SIMPLE plan, or a simplified employee pension (SEP). The credit applies to 50 percent of the first $1,000 in administrative and retirement-education expenses for the plan for each of the first three years of the plan.

The credit is available to an employer that did not employ, in the preceding year, more than 100 employees with compensation in excess of $5,000. In order for an employer to be eligible for the credit, the plan must cover at least one non–highly compensated employee. In addition, if the credit is for the cost of a payroll-deduction IRA arrangement, the arrangement must be made available to all employees of the employer who have worked with the employer for at least three months.

The credit is a general business credit and cannot be carried back to years before 2002. Also, the expenses that qualify for the credit cannot also be offset by a tax deduction.

Contributions of Employees to Defined Contribution Plans

Pre-2001 Tax Act

Limits are imposed on the contributions that may be made to tax-favored retirement plans. In the case of a defined contribution plan, the limit on annual additions that can be made to the plan on behalf of an employee is the lesser of $35,000 (for 2001) or 25 percent of the employee's compensation under Section 415(c). In the case of a tax-sheltered 403(b) annuity, the annual contribution generally cannot exceed the lesser of the exclusion allowance or the Section 415(c) defined contribution limit. The exclusion allowance for a year is equal to 20 percent of the employee's includable compensation, multiplied by the employee's years of service, minus excludable contributions for prior years under qualified plans, tax-sheltered annuities, or 457 plans of the employer. Compensation deferred under an eligible deferred compensation plan of a tax-exempt or state and local governmental employer (a 457 plan) is not includable in gross income until paid or made available. In general, the maximum permitted annual deferral under such a plan is the lesser of (1) $8,500 (in 2001) or (2) $33\frac{1}{3}$ percent of compensation. The $8,500 limit is increased for inflation in $500 increments.

New Law

TIP

Another provision, discussed earlier in this chapter, increases the defined contribution plan dollar limit to $40,000 from $35,000.

After 2001, the 25 percent of compensation limitation on annual additions under a defined contribution plan are increased to 100 percent.

The exclusion allowance for contributions to tax-sheltered annuities is repealed. Thus, 403(b) annuities are subject to the limits applicable to tax-qualified plans.

For tax years beginning after 1999, a plan may elect to disregard the requirement that contributions to a defined benefit plan be treated as previously excluded amounts for purposes of the 403(b) exclusion allowance.

The 33⅓ percent of compensation limit on deferrals to a 457 plan is increased to 100 percent of compensation.

Distributions after Separation from Service

Pre-2001 Tax Act

Elective deferrals under a 401(k) plan, a tax-sheltered 403(b) annuity, or an eligible Section 457 deferred compensation plan of a tax-exempt organization or state or local government may not be distributable prior to the occurrence of one or more specified events. One permissible distributable event is "separation from service."

A separation from service occurs only upon a participant's death, retirement, resignation, or discharge, and not when the employee continues on the same job for a different employer as a result of the liquidation, merger, consolidation, or other similar corporate transaction. A severance from employment occurs when a participant ceases to be employed by the employer that maintains the plan. Under a so-called same-desk rule, a participant's severance from employment does not necessarily result in a separation from service.

In addition to separation from service and other events, a 401(k) plan that is maintained by a corporation may permit distributions to certain employees who experience a severance from employment with the corporation that maintains the plan but do not experience a separation from service because the employees continue on the same job for a different employer as a result of a corporate transaction. If the corporation disposes of substantially all of the assets used by the corporation in a trade or business, a distributable event occurs with respect to the accounts of the employees who

TIP

Under a recent IRS ruling, a person is generally deemed to have separated from service if that person is transferred to another employer in connection with a sale of less than substantially all the assets of a trade or business.

Under the same-desk rule, if a company is involved in a liquidation, consolidation, or merger, no separation from service would occur when an employee stops working for the predecessor employer and works for the postreorganization employer if the employee's job remains the same.

continue employment with the corporation that acquires the assets. If the corporation disposes of its interest in a subsidiary, a distributable event occurs with respect to the accounts of the employees who continue employment with the subsidiary.

New Law

TIP

The same-desk rule is generally eliminated with respect to distributions from 401(k) plans, 403(b) annuities, and 457 plans.

Distributions after 2001 from 401(k) plans, 403(b) annuities, and 457 plans generally may occur upon severance from employment rather than separation from service. The provisions for distributions from a 401(k) plan based on a corporation's disposition of its assets or a subsidiary are repealed as they are no longer necessary.

However, the Conference Report noted that a plan might provide that certain types of severance from employment do not constitute distributable events. For example, a plan could provide that a severance from employment is not a distributable event if it would not have constituted a "separation from service" under prior law.

The Conference Report also noted that, as under prior law, if there is a transfer of plan assets and liabilities relating to any portion of an employee's benefit under a plan of the employee's former employer to a plan being maintained or created by the employee's new employer (other than a rollover or elective transfer), then that employee has not experienced a severance from employment with the employer maintaining the plan that covers the employee.

Employers May Disregard Rollovers for Purposes of Cash-Out Rules

Pre-2001 Tax Act

If a qualified retirement plan participant ceases to be employed by the employer that maintains the plan, the plan may distribute the participant's nonforfeitable accrued benefit without the consent of the participant and, if applicable, the participant's spouse, if the present value of the benefit does not exceed $5,000. If such an involuntary distribution occurs and the participant subsequently returns to employment covered by the plan, then service taken into account in computing benefits payable under the plan after the return need not include service with respect to which a benefit was involuntarily distributed unless the employee repays the benefit.

Generally, a participant may roll over an involuntary distribution from a qualified plan to an IRA or to another qualified plan.

TIP

Other provisions, discussed above, expand the kinds of plans to which benefits may be rolled over.

New Law

For distributions after 2001, a plan is permitted to provide, for purposes of the cash-out rule, that the present value of a

TIP

The effect of this provision is to allow an employer to "cash-out" an employee involuntarily without having to take into account amounts rolled over from another plan.

participant's nonforfeitable accrued benefit is determined without regard to the portion of such benefit that is attributable to rollover contributions (and any earnings allocable thereto).

Investment of Employee Contributions in 401(k) Plans

Pre-2001 Tax Act

ERISA prohibits certain employee benefit plans from acquiring securities or real property of the employer who sponsors the plan if, after the acquisition, the fair market value of such securities and property exceeds 10 percent of the fair market value of plan assets. The 10 percent limitation does not apply to any "eligible individual account plans" that specifically authorize such investments. Generally, eligible individual account plans are defined contribution plans, including plans containing a cash or deferred arrangement such as 401(k) plans.

The term "eligible individual account plan" does not include the portion of a plan that consists of elective deferrals (and earnings on the elective deferrals) made under 401(k) if elective deferrals equal to more than 1 percent of any employee's eligible compensation are required to be invested in employer securities and employer real property. Eligible compensation is compensation that is eligible to be deferred under the plan. The portion of the plan that consists of elective deferrals (and earnings thereon) is still treated as an individual account plan, and the 10 percent limitation does not apply, as long as elective deferrals (and earnings thereon) are not required to be invested in employer securities or employer real property.

The rule excluding elective deferrals (and earnings thereon) from the definition of eligible individual account plan applies to elective deferrals for plan years beginning after December 31, 1998.

New Law

The effective date of the rule excluding certain elective deferrals (and earnings thereon) from the definition of eligible individual account plan is modified by providing that the rule does not apply to any elective deferral used to acquire an interest in the income or gain from employer securities or employer real property acquired (1) before January 1, 1999, or (2) after such date pursuant to a written contract that was binding on such date and at all times thereafter.

This provision is effective as if included in the section of the Taxpayer Relief Act of 1997 that contained the rule excluding certain elective deferrals (and earnings thereon). The effective date, as originally enacted by the Taxpayer Relief Act of 1997, inadvertently applied the 10 percent test to elective deferrals before 1999, even if the elective deferrals were invested before 1999 causing complexity in plan record keeping.

Treatment of Employer-Provided Retirement Advice

Pre-2001 Tax Act

Certain employer-provided fringe benefits are excludable from gross income and wages for employment tax purposes. These excludable fringe benefits include working-condition fringe benefits and *de minimis* fringes.

In addition, certain employer-provided educational assistance is excludable from income. There is no specific exclusion for employer-provided retirement planning services.

> Generally, a working-condition fringe benefit is any property or service provided by an employer to an employee to the extent that, if the employee paid for such property or service, such payment would be allowable as a deduction as a business expense. A *de minimis* fringe benefit is any property or service provided by the employer the value of which, after taking into account the frequency with which similar fringes are provided, is so small as to make accounting for it unreasonable or administratively impracticable.

New Law

After 2001, qualified retirement planning services provided to an employee and his or her spouse by an employer maintaining a qualified plan are excludable from income and wages. The exclusion does not apply with respect to highly compensated employees unless the services are available on substantially the same terms to each member of the group of employees normally provided education and information regarding the employer's qualified plan. "Qualified retirement planning services" are retirement planning advice and information. The exclusion is not limited to information regarding the qualified plan, and thus, for example, it applies to advice and information regarding retirement income planning for an individual and his or her spouse and how the employer's plan fits into the individual's overall retirement income plan. However, the exclusion does not apply to tax preparation, accounting, legal, or brokerage services.

TIP

Retirement advice should be provided in a nondiscriminatory manner. However, employers may take into account circumstances other than compensation and position for purposes of providing advice. For example, advice may be limited to those nearing retirement age.

APPENDIX

Overview

During the presidential campaign, there was a great deal of discussion about candidate Bush's proposed tax bill. How much would it cost? Who would benefit most?

We've provided a set of tables that gives the reader the opportunity to review some of the material provided by the nonpartisan Congressional Joint Committee on Taxation, which set out to answer just such questions.

One of the cornerstones of the new tax law is the rate reduction. Table A.1 provides a history of federal individual income tax rates for the bottom and the top tax brackets. This should help you to put things into perspective. It is interesting to note that at one time, the top federal rate was 94 percent (1944–1945), and the lowest rate was as low as 1 percent (1913–1915, 1925–1928, 1930–1931).

When considering the rate reductions, it is a good idea

to gain an understanding of the distribution of the federal income tax liability among individuals. Table A.2 shows just this. The highest tax bracket pays an overwhelming majority of the tax liability (47.5 percent), while accounting for a very small percentage of total filers (2.7 percent). At the same time, the largest percentage of tax filers (16.4 percent) actually pays for –1 percent of the tax liability. This is the root of the criticism that the new tax law favors the wealthy. Indeed it is hard to cut income taxes for those who do not actually pay any taxes. As far as arguing the social justice of this policy is concerned, we leave that to the reader.

So who gets the majority of the tax cut? Tables A.3a through A.3f provide the reader with the answer for tax years 2001 through 2006. The answer may be surprising after reviewing Table A.2. The same group that accounted for the highest percentage of filers in Table A.2 (which paid for –1 percent of the tax liability) actually receives the highest *percentage* of the tax cut in 2001 (11.5 percent). This is somewhat deceiving. As with all good statistics, the answers can be manipulated in many ways. If considered in dollar terms, the $50,000 to $75,000 group actually receives the greatest amount of the tax cut in 2001. But remember that many of these tax cuts are phased in. If you skip to Table A.3f, you'll see a somewhat different picture. The same group again gets the largest percentage tax cut, but look at the dollar value of the cuts for the two highest income levels. They receive over 54 percent of the dollar value of the tax cut. Again, we leave the arguments up to you.

Finally, the Appendix addresses the question, "How much does the tax bill cost?" Spread out over many pages, Table

A.4 takes the reader through every provision of the tax bill and outlines the cost for each year (from 2001 to 2011). The amounts are totaled at the far right of the spreadsheet for the periods 2001 to 2006 and 2001 to 2011. What is interesting to see is that the most expensive provision of the tax code is the reduction of the marginal tax rates. Over the lifetime of the plan, these cuts will account for 64 percent of the total cost. Interestingly, the more controversial estate tax repeal will account for only a little over 10 percent of the costs.

TABLE A.1 History of Federal Individual Income Bottom and Top Bracket Rates

| Calendar Year | Tax Rates[1] | | | |
| | Bottom Bracket | | Top Bracket | |
	Rate (Percent)	Taxable Income Up To	Rate (Percent)	Taxable Income Over
1913–1915	1%	$20,000	7%	$ 500,000
1916	2	20,000	15	2,000,000
1917	2	2,000	67	2,000,000
1918	6	4,000	77	1,000,000
1919-1920	4	4,000	73	1,000,000
1921	4	4,000	73	1,000,000
1922	4	4,000	56	200,000
1923	3	4,000	56	200,000
1924	1.5[2]	4,000	46	500,000
1925–1928	1[2]	4,000	25	100,000
1929	4[2]	4,000	24	100,000
1930–1931	1[2]	4,000	25	100,000
1932–1933	4	4,000	63	1,000,000
1934–1935	4[3]	4,000	63	1,000,000
1936–1939	4[3]	4,000	79	5,000,000
1940	4.4[3]	4,000	81.1	5,000,000
1941	10[3]	2,000	81	5,000,000
1942-1943[3]	19[3]	2,000	88	200,000
1944–1945	23	2,000	94[5]	200,000
1946–1947	19	2,000	86.45[5]	200,000
1948–1949	16.6	4,000	82.13[5]	400,000
1950	17.4	4,000	91[5]	400,000

TABLE A.1 *(Continued)*

| Calendar Year | Tax Rates[1] | | | |
| | Bottom Bracket | | Top Bracket | |
	Rate (Percent)	Taxable Income Up To	Rate (Percent)	Taxable Income Over
1951	20.4	4,000	91[5]	400,000
1952–1953	22.2	4,000	92[5]	400,000
1954–1963	20	4,000	91[5]	400,000
1964	16	1,000	77	400,000
1965–1967	14	1,000	70	200,000
1968	14	1,000	75.25[6]	200,000
1969	14	1,000	77[6]	200,000
1970	14	1,000	71.75[6]	200,000
1971	14	1,000	70[7]	200,000
1972–1978	14[8]	1,000	70[7]	200,000
1979–1980	14[8]	2,100	70[7]	212,000
1981	13.825[8,9]	2,100	69.125[7,9]	212,000
1982	12[8]	2,100	50	106,000
1983	11[8]	2,100	50	106,000
1984	11[8]	2,100	50	159,000
1985	11[8]	2,180	50	165,480
1986	11[8]	2,270	50	171,580
1987	11[8]	3,000	38.5	90,000
1988	15[8]	29,750	28[10]	29,750
1989	15[8]	30,950	28[10]	30,950
1990	15[8]	32,450	28[10]	32,450
1991	15[8]	34,000	31	82,150
1992	15[8]	35,800	31	86,500

TABLE A.1 *(Continued)*

Calendar Year	TAX RATES[1] Bottom Bracket Rate (Percent)	Taxable Income Up To	Top Bracket Rate (Percent)	Taxable Income Over
1993	15[8]	36,900	39.6	250,000
1994	15[8]	38,000	39.6	250,000
1995	15[8]	39,000	39.6	256,500
1996	15[8]	40,100	39.6	263,750
1997	15[8]	41,200	39.6	271,050
1998	15[8]	42,350	39.6	278,450
1999	15[8]	43050	39.6	283,150
2000	15[8]	43,850	39.6	288,350

1. Taxable income excludes zero bracket amount from 1977 through 1986. Rates shown apply only to married persons filing joint returns beginning in 1948. Does not include either the add-on minimum tax on preference items (1970 to 1982) or the alternative minimum tax (1979 to the present). Also, does not include the effects of the various tax benefit phaseouts (e.g., the personal exemption phaseout). From 1922 through 1986 and from 1991 forward, lower rates applied to long-term capital gains.
2. After earned-income deduction equal to 25 percent of earned income.
3. After earned-income deduction equal to 10 percent of earned income.
4. Exclusive of Victory Tax.
5. Subject to the following maximum effective rate limitations: 1944 to 1945—90 percent; 1946 to 1947—85.5 percent; 1948 to 1949—77 percent; 1950—87 percent; 1951—87.2 percent; 1952 to 1953—88 percent; 1954 to 1963—87 percent.
6. Includes surcharge of 7.5 percent in 1968, 10 percent in 1969, and 2.6 percent in 1970.
7. Earned income was subject to maximum marginal rates of 60 percent in 1971 and 50 percent from 1972 through 1981.
8. Beginning in 1975, a refundable earned income credit is allowed for low-income individuals.
9. After-tax credit is 1.25 percent against regular tax.
10. The benefit of the first rate bracket is eliminated by an increased rate above certain thresholds. The phaseout range of the benefit of the first rate bracket was as follows: Taxable income between $71,900 and $149,250 in 1988; taxable income between $74,850 and $155,320 in 1989; and taxable income between $78,400 and $162,770 in 1990. The phaseout of the benefit of the first rate bracket was repealed for taxable years beginning after December 31, 1990. This added 5 percentage points to the marginal rate for those affected by the phaseout, producing a 33 percent effective rate.

Source: Joint Committee on Taxation.

TABLE A.2 Distribution of Federal Individual Income Tax Liability, Calendar Year 2001[1]

INCOME CATEGORY[2]	NUMBER OF RETURNS[3]		INCOME		INDIVIDUAL INCOME TAX		NUMBER OF RETURNS WITH ZERO OR NEGATIVE LIABILITY	
	MILLIONS	PERCENT	BILLIONS	PERCENT	BILLIONS	PERCENT	MILLIONS	PERCENT
Less than $10,000	19.9	14.0%	$ 83	1.0%	–$ 6	–0.6%	18.8	38.7%
$10,000 to $20,000	23.3	16.4%	$ 347	4.2%	–$ 10	–1.0%	16.2	33.3%
$20,000 to $30,000	18.5	13.0%	$ 460	5.6%	$ 9	0.9%	8.1	16.6%
$30,000 to $40,000	15.8	11.1%	$ 549	6.7%	$ 28	2.8%	3.2	6.6%
$40,000 to $50,000	13.1	9.2%	$ 589	7.2%	$ 39	3.9%	1.4	3.0%
$50,000 to $75,000	21.9	15.4%	$1,337	16.4%	$ 112	11.1%	0.8	1.6%
$75,000 to $100,000	12.9	9.1%	$1,121	13.7%	$ 119	11.8%	0.1	0.1%

$100,000 to $200,000	12.8	9.0%	$1,683	20.6%	$ 237	23.6%	<0.05	0.1%
$200,000 and over	3.8	2.7%	$1,999	24.5%	$ 478	47.5%	<0.05	<0.005%
Total, All Taxpayers	142.0	100.0%	$8,168	100.0%	$1,006	100.0%	48.6	100.0%
Highest 10%	14.2	10.0%	$3,431	42.0%	$ 686	68.2%	<0.05	0.1%
Highest 5%	7.1	5.0%	$2,556	31.3%	570	56.6%	<0.05	<0.005%
Highest 1%	1.4	1.0%	$1,402	17.2%	361	35.9%	<0.05	<0.005%

Detail may not add to total due to rounding.

1. Includes the outlay portion of the earned income credit (EIC).
2. The income concept used to place tax returns into income categories is adjusted gross income (AGI) plus: (1) tax-exempt interest, (2) employer contributions for health plans and life insurance, (3) employer share of FICA tax, (4) workers' compensation, (5) nontaxable Social Security benefits, (6) insurance value of Medicare benefits, (7) alternative minimum tax preference items, and (8) excluded income of U.S. citizens living abroad. Categories are measured at 2001 levels. The highest 10 percent begins at $107,455, the highest 5 percent at $145,199, and the highest 1 percent at $340,306.
3. Includes filing and nonfiling units. Individuals who are dependents of other taxpayers and taxpayers with negative income are excluded.

Source: Joint Committee on Taxation.

TABLE A.3a Distributional Effects of the Conference Agreement for H.R. 1836, Calendar Year 2001[1]

INCOME CATEGORY[2]	CHANGES IN FEDERAL TAXES[3]		FEDERAL TAXES[3] UNDER PRESENT LAW		FEDERAL TAXES[3] UNDER PROPOSAL		EFFECTIVE TAX RATE[4]	
							PRESENT LAW	PROPOSAL
	MILLIONS	PERCENT	BILLIONS	PERCENT	BILLIONS	PERCENT	PERCENT	PERCENT
Less than $10,000	-$ 75	-1.0%	$ 7	0.4%	$ 7	0.4%	8.7%	8.6%
$10,000 to $20,000	-$ 2989	-11.5%	$ 26	1.5%	$ 23	1.4%	7.5%	6.7%
$20,000 to $30,000	-$ 5,790	-9.4%	$ 62	3.5%	$ 56	3.3%	13.4%	12.2%
$30,000 to $40,000	-$ 5,674	-6.4%	$ 89	5.1%	$ 83	4.9%	16.1%	15.1%
$40,000 to $50,000	-$ 5,490	-5.4%	$ 102	5.9%	$ 97	5.7%	17.4%	16.4%
$50,000 to $75,000	-$11,546	-4.5%	$ 256	14.6%	$ 244	14.4%	19.1%	18.3%
$75,000 to $100,000	-$ 8,488	-3.5%	$ 244	13.9%	$ 235	13.9%	21.7%	21.0%
$100,000 to $200,000	-$10,488	-2.6%	$ 408	23.3%	$ 397	23.5%	24.2%	23.6%
$200,000 and over	-$ 6,997	-1.3%	$ 555	31.7%	$ 548	32.4%	27.8%	27.4%
Total, All Taxpayers	-$57,536	-3.3%	$1,748	100.0%	$1,690	100.0%	21.4%	20.7%

Note: Detail may not add to total due to rounding.
1. Includes provisions affecting the child credit, individual marginal rates, a 10 percent bracket, limitation of itemized deductions, the personal exemption phaseout, the standard deduction, 15 percent bracket and EIC for married couples deductible IRAs, and the AMT.
2. The income concept used to place tax returns into income categories is adjusted gross income (AGI) plus: (1) tax-exempt interest, (2) employer contributions for health plans and life insurance, (3) employer share of FICA tax, (4) workers' compensation, (5) nontaxable Social Security benefits, (6) insurance value of Medicare benefits, (7) alternative minimum tax preference items, and (8) excluded income of U.S. citizens living abroad. Categories are measured at 2001 levels.
3. Federal taxes are equal to individual income tax (including the outlay portion of the EIC), employment tax (attributed to employees), and excise taxes (attributed to consumers). Corporate income tax and estate and gift taxes are not included due to uncertainty concerning the incidence of these taxes. Individuals who are dependents of other taxpayers and taxpayers with negative income are excluded from the analysis. Does not include indirect effects.
4. The effective tax rate is equal to federal taxes described in footnote 3 divided by: income described in footnote 2 plus additional income attributable to the proposal.
Source: Joint Committee on Taxation.

TABLE A.3b Distributional Effects of the Conference Agreement for H.R. 1836, Calendar Year 2002[1]

| INCOME CATEGORY[2] | CHANGES IN FEDERAL TAXES[3] | | FEDERAL TAXES[3] UNDER PRESENT LAW | | FEDERAL TAXES[3] UNDER PROPOSAL | | EFFECTIVE TAX RATE[4] | |
	MILLIONS	PERCENT	BILLIONS	PERCENT	BILLIONS	PERCENT	PRESENT LAW PERCENT	PROPOSAL PERCENT
Less than $10,000	–$ 75	–1.0%	$ 7	0.4%	$ 7	0.4%	9.2%	9.1%
$10,000 to $20,000	–$ 3,596	–13.3%	$ 27	1.5%	$ 23	1.3%	7.6%	6.6%
$20,000 to $30,000	–$ 7,124	–11.3%	$ 63	3.4%	$ 56	3.2%	13.5%	12.0%
$30,000 to $40,000	–$ 6,849	–7.6%	$ 91	4.9%	$ 84	4.8%	16.1%	14.8%
$40,000 to $50,000	–$ 6,198	–5.8%	$ 106	5.8%	$ 100	5.7%	17.5%	16.5%
$50,000 to $75,000	–$13,251	–5.0%	$ 267	14.5%	$ 254	14.4%	19.0%	18.0%
$75,000 to $100,000	–$10,227	–4.0%	$ 255	13.9%	$ 245	13.9%	21.7%	20.8%
$100,000 to $200,000	–$14,416	–3.3%	$ 442	24.1%	$ 427	24.3%	24.2%	23.4%
$200,000 and over	–$16,557	–2.9%	$ 578	31.5%	$ 562	32.0%	27.9%	27.1%
Total, All Taxpayers	–$78,294	–4.3%	$1,836	100.0%	$1,758	100.0%	21.5%	20.6%

Note: Detail may not add to total due to rounding.
1. Includes provisions affecting the child credit, individual marginal rates, a 10 percent bracket, limitation of itemized deductions, the personal exemption phaseout, the standard deduction, 15 percent bracket and EIC for married couples deductible IRAs, and the AMT.
2. The income concept used to place tax returns into income categories is adjusted gross income (AGI) plus: (1) tax-exempt interest, (2) employer contributions for health plans and life insurance, (3) employer share of FICA tax, (4) workers' compensation, (5) nontaxable Social Security benefits, (6) insurance value of Medicare benefits, (7) alternative minimum tax preference items, and (8) excluded income of U.S. citizens living abroad. Categories are measured at 2001 levels.
3. Federal taxes are equal to individual income tax (including the outlay portion of the EIC), employment tax (attributed to employees), and excise taxes (attributed to consumers). Corporate income tax and estate and gift taxes are not included due to uncertainty concerning the incidence of these taxes. Individuals who are dependents of other taxpayers and taxpayers with negative income are excluded from the analysis. Does not include indirect effects.
4. The effective tax rate is equal to federal taxes described in footnote 3 divided by: income described in footnote 2 plus additional income attributable to the proposal.
Source: Joint Committee on Taxation.

TABLE A.3c Distributional Effects of the Conference Agreement for H.R. 1836, Calendar Year 2003[1]

INCOME CATEGORY[2]	CHANGES IN FEDERAL TAXES[3]		FEDERAL TAXES[3] UNDER PRESENT LAW		FEDERAL TAXES[3] UNDER PROPOSAL		EFFECTIVE TAX RATE[4]	
	MILLIONS	PERCENT	BILLIONS	PERCENT	BILLIONS	PERCENT	PRESENT LAW PERCENT	PROPOSAL PERCENT
Less than $10,000	–$ 83	–1.1%	$ 8	0.4%	$ 8	0.4%	9.7%	9.6%
$10,000 to $20,000	–$ 3,516	–12.9%	$ 27	1.4%	$ 24	1.3%	7.6%	6.6%
$20,000 to $30,000	–$ 7,135	–11.0%	$ 65	3.3%	$ 58	3.1%	13.6%	12.1%
$30,000 to $40,000	–$ 6,946	–7.5%	$ 93	4.8%	$ 86	4.6%	16.0%	14.8%
$40,000 to $50,000	–$ 6,155	–5.7%	$ 108	5.6%	$ 101	5.5%	17.4%	16.4%
$50,000 to $75,000	–$13,554	–4.9%	$ 279	14.4%	$ 266	14.3%	18.9.%	18.0%
$75,000 to $100,000	–$10,553	–4.0%	$ 265	13.7%	$ 255	13.8%	21.7%	20.8%
$100,000 to $200,000	–$15,487	–3.2%	$ 479	24.8%	$ 464	25.1%	24.2%	23.4%
$200,000 and over	–$17,453	–2.9%	$ 609	31.5%	$ 591	31.9%	28.1%	27.3%
Total, All Taxpayers	–$80,882	–4.2%	$1,933	100.0%	$1,852	100.0%	21.5%	20.6%

Note: Detail may not add to total due to rounding.
1. Includes provisions affecting the child credit, individual marginal rates, a 10 percent bracket, limitation of itemized deductions, the personal exemption phaseout, the standard deduction, 15 percent bracket and EIC for married couples deductible IRAs, and the AMT.
2. The income concept used to place tax returns into income categories is adjusted gross income (AGI) plus: (1) tax-exempt interest, (2) employer contributions for health plans and life insurance, (3) employer share of FICA tax, (4) workers' compensation, (5) nontaxable Social Security benefits, (6) insurance value of Medicare benefits, (7) alternative minimum tax preference items, and (8) excluded income of U.S. citizens living abroad. Categories are measured at 2001 levels.
3. Federal taxes are equal to individual income tax (including the outlay portion of the EIC), employment tax (attributed to employees), and excise taxes (attributed to consumers). Corporate income tax and estate and gift taxes are not included due to uncertainty concerning the incidence of these taxes. Individuals who are dependents of other taxpayers and taxpayers with negative income are excluded from the analysis. Does not include indirect effects.
4. The effective tax rate is equal to federal taxes described in footnote 3 divided by: income described in footnote 2 plus additional income attributable to the proposal.
Source: Joint Committee on Taxation.

TABLE A.3d Distributional Effects of the Conference Agreement for H.R. 1836, Calendar Year 2004[1]

| INCOME CATEGORY[2] | CHANGES IN FEDERAL TAXES[3] | | FEDERAL TAXES[3] UNDER PRESENT LAW | | FEDERAL TAXES[3] UNDER PROPOSAL | | EFFECTIVE TAX RATE[4] | |
| | | | | | | | PRESENT LAW | PROPOSAL |
	MILLIONS	PERCENT	BILLIONS	PERCENT	BILLIONS	PERCENT	PERCENT	PERCENT
Less than $10,000	-$ 69	-0.9%	$ 8	0.4%	$ 8	0.4%	10.0%	9.9%
$10,000 to $20,000	-$ 3,429	-12.6%	$ 27	1.3%	$ 24	1.2%	7.6%	6.6%
$20,000 to $30,000	-$ 7,121	-11.8%	$ 66	3.3%	$ 59	3.1%	13.6%	12.2%
$30,000 to $40,000	-$ 6,964	-7.3%	$ 96	4.7%	$ 89	4.6%	16.0%	14.8%
$40,000 to $50,000	-$ 6,320	-5.8%	$ 110	5.4%	$ 103	5.3%	17.4%	16.4%
$50,000 to $75,000	-$15,049	-5.2%	$ 288	14.2%	$ 273	14.2%	18.7%	17.8%
$75,000 to $100,000	-$12,913	-4.6%	$ 279	13.8%	$ 266	13.8%	21.5%	20.5%
$100,000 to $200,000	-$22,095	-4.3%	$ 512	25.2%	$ 490	25.3%	24.1%	23.0%
$200,000 and over	-$21,671	-3.4%	$ 642	31.6%	$ 620	32.1%	28.2%	27.3%
Total, All Taxpayers	-$95,630	-4.7%	$2,028	100.0%	$1,932	100.0%	21.6%	20.6%

Note: Detail may not add to total due to rounding.
1. Includes provisions affecting the child credit, individual marginal rates, a 10 percent bracket, limitation of itemized deductions, the personal exemption phaseout, the standard deduction, 15 percent bracket and EIC for married couples deductible IRAs, and the AMT.
2. The income concept used to place tax returns into income categories is adjusted gross income (AGI) plus: (1) tax-exempt interest, (2) employer contributions for health plans and life insurance, (3) employer share of FICA tax, (4) workers' compensation, (5) nontaxable Social Security benefits, (6) insurance value of Medicare benefits, (7) alternative minimum tax preference items, and (8) excluded income of U.S. citizens living abroad. Categories are measured at 2001 levels.
3. Federal taxes are equal to individual income tax (including the outlay portion of the EIC), employment tax (attributed to employees), and excise taxes (attributed to consumers). Corporate income tax and estate and gift taxes are not included due to uncertainty concerning the incidence of these taxes. Individuals who are dependents of other taxpayers and taxpayers with negative income are excluded from the analysis. Does not include indirect effects.
4. The effective tax rate is equal to federal taxes described in footnote 3 divided by: income described in footnote 2 plus additional income attributable to the proposal.
Source: Joint Committee on Taxation.

TABLE A.3e Distributional Effects of the Conference Agreement for H.R. 1836, Calendar Year 2005[1]

| INCOME CATEGORY[2] | CHANGES IN FEDERAL TAXES[3] | | FEDERAL TAXES[3] UNDER PRESENT LAW | | FEDERAL TAXES[3] UNDER PROPOSAL | | EFFECTIVE TAX RATE[4] | |
| | | | | | | | PRESENT LAW | PROPOSAL |
	MILLIONS	PERCENT	BILLIONS	PERCENT	BILLIONS	PERCENT	PERCENT	PERCENT
Less than $10,000	-$ 76	-1.0%	$ 8	0.4%	$ 8	0.4%	10.1%	10.0%
$10,000 to $20,000	-$ 3,867	-14.0%	$ 28	1.3%	$ 24	1.2%	7.6%	6.5%
$20,000 to $30,000	-$ 7,937	-11.6%	$ 68	3.2%	$ 60	3.0%	13.7%	12.1%
$30,000 to $40,000	-$ 7,720	-7.9%	$ 98	4.6%	$ 90	4.4%	16.0%	14.7%
$40,000 to $50,000	-$ 6,945	-6.2%	$ 112	5.3%	$ 105	5.2%	17.2%	16.2%
$50,000 to $75,000	-$ 16,630	-5.5%	$ 303	14.2%	$ 286	14.1%	18.7%	17.6%
$75,000 to $100,000	-$ 14,709	-5.1%	$ 287	13.5%	$ 273	13.5%	21.4%	20.3%
$100,000 to $200,000	-$ 24,654	-4.5%	$ 547	25.7%	$ 522	25.8%	24.0%	22.9%
$200,000 and over	-$ 21,182	-3.1%	$ 678	31.9%	$ 657	32.4%	28.3%	27.4%
Total, All Taxpayers	-$103,720	-4.9%	$2,129	100.0%	$2,025	100.0%	21.6%	20.6%

Note: Detail may not add to total due to rounding.

1. Includes provisions affecting the child credit, individual marginal rates, a 10 percent bracket, limitation of itemized deductions, the personal exemption phaseout, the standard deduction, 15 percent bracket and EIC for married couples deductible IRAs, and the AMT.
2. The income concept used to place tax returns into income categories is adjusted gross income (AGI) plus: (1) tax-exempt interest, (2) employer contributions for health plans and life insurance, (3) employer share of FICA tax, (4) workers' compensation, (5) nontaxable Social Security benefits, (6) insurance value of Medicare benefits, (7) alternative minimum tax preference items, and (8) excluded income of U.S. citizens living abroad. Categories are measured at 2001 levels.
3. Federal taxes are equal to individual income tax (including the outlay portion of the EIC), employment tax (attributed to employees), and excise taxes (attributed to consumers). Corporate income tax and estate and gift taxes are not included due to uncertainty concerning the incidence of these taxes. Individuals who are dependents of other taxpayers and taxpayers with negative income are excluded from the analysis. Does not include indirect effects.
4. The effective tax rate is equal to federal taxes described in footnote 3 divided by: income described in footnote 2 plus additional income attributable to the proposal.
Source: Joint Committee on Taxation.

TABLE A.3f Distributional Effects of the Conference Agreement for H.R. 1836, Calendar Year 2006[1]

INCOME CATEGORY[2]	CHANGES IN FEDERAL TAXES[3]		FEDERAL TAXES[3] UNDER PRESENT LAW		FEDERAL TAXES[3] UNDER PROPOSAL		EFFECTIVE TAX RATE[4]	
	MILLIONS	PERCENT	BILLIONS	PERCENT	BILLIONS	PERCENT	PRESENT LAW PERCENT	PROPOSAL PERCENT
Less than $10,000	-$ 76	-0.9%	$ 8	0.4%	$ 8	0.4%	10.4%	10.3%
$10,000 to $20,000	-$ 3,789	-13.6%	$ 28	1.2%	$ 24	1.1%	7.6%	6.6%
$20,000 to $30,000	-$ 7,853	-11.4%	$ 69	3.1%	$ 61	2.9%	13.7%	12.2%
$30,000 to $40,000	-$ 7,839	-7.9%	$ 99	4.4%	$ 91	4.4%	16.0%	14.7%
$40,000 to $50,000	-$ 7,570	-6.5%	$ 116	5.2%	$ 108	5.2%	17.2%	16.0%
$50,000 to $75,000	-$ 18,755	-6.0%	$ 313	14.0%	$ 294	14.0%	18.6%	17.5%
$75,000 to $100,000	-$ 17,212	-5.8%	$ 297	13.3%	$ 280	13.3%	21.3%	20.0%
$100,000 to $200,000	-$ 30,208	-5.1%	$ 588	26.3%	$ 558	26.6%	23.9%	22.7%
$200,000 and over	-$ 44,177	-6.1%	$ 719	32.1%	$ 675	32.1%	28.3%	26.6%
Total, All Taxpayers	-$137,476	-6.1%	$2,238	100.0%	$2,100	100.0%	21.7%	20.3%

Note: Detail may not add to total due to rounding.
1. Includes provisions affecting the child credit, individual marginal rates, a 10 percent bracket, limitation of itemized deductions, the personal exemption phaseout, the standard deduction, 15 percent bracket and EIC for married couples deductible IRAs, and the AMT.
2. The income concept used to place tax returns into income categories is adjusted gross income (AGI) plus: (1) tax-exempt interest, (2) employer contributions for health plans and life insurance, (3) employer share of FICA tax, (4) workers' compensation, (5) nontaxable Social Security benefits, (6) insurance value of Medicare benefits, (7) alternative minimum tax preference items, and (8) excluded income of U.S. citizens living abroad. Categories are measured at 2001 levels.
3. Federal taxes are equal to individual income tax (including the outlay portion of the EIC), employment tax (attributed to employees), and excise taxes (attributed to consumers). Corporate income tax and estate and gift taxes are not included due to uncertainty concerning the incidence of these taxes. Individuals who are dependents of other taxpayers and taxpayers with negative income are excluded from the analysis. Does not include indirect effects.
4. The effective tax rate is equal to federal taxes described in footnote 3 divided by: income described in footnote 2 plus additional income attributable to the proposal.
Source: Joint Committee on Taxation.

TABLE A.4 Estimated Budget Effects of the Conference Agreement for H.R. 1836, Fiscal Years 2001 to 2011 (Millions of Dollars)[1]

PROVISION	EFFECTIVE	2001	2002	2003
Marginal Rate Reduction Provisions (Sunset 12/31/10)				
1. Create new 10% bracket in 2001 through 2007 for the first $6,000 of taxable income for singles, first $10,000 for heads of households, and first $12,000 for married couples, and in 2008, first $7,000 of taxable income for singles, first $10,000 for heads of households, and first $14,000 for married couples; and index beginning in 2009; credit with advanced payment in lieu of rate for 2001	tyba 12/31/00	−38,186	−33,421	−40,223
2. Reduce the various income tax rates (39.6% rate reduced to 38.6% in 2001 through 2003, 37.6% in 2004 and 2005, 35% in 2001 through 2003, and 34% in 2004 and 2005, and 33% in 2006 and thereafter; 31% rate reduced to 30% in 2001 through 2003, 29% in 2004 and 2005, 28% in 2006 and thereafter, 28% rate reduced to 27% in 2001 through 2003, 26% in 2004 and 2005, and 25% in 2006 and thereafter)	7/1/01	−2,005	−21,100	−21,256
3. Phase in repeal of Pease cutback of itemized deductions over 5 years	tyba 12/31/05	—	—	—
4. Phase in repeal of the personal exemption phaseout over 5 years	tyba 12/31/05	—	—	—
Total of Marginal Rate Reduction Provisions (Sunset 12/31/10)		−40,191	−54,521	−61,479
Increase the Child Tax Credit from $500 to $600 in 2001 through 2004, $700 in 2005 through 2008, $800 in 2009, and $1,000 in 2010; Make Refundable up to Greater of 15% (10% for 2001 through 2004) of Earned Income in Excess of $10,000 (Indexed in 2002) or Present Law; Allow Credit Permanently Against the AMT; Repeal AMT Offset of Refundable Credits; Sunset 12/31/10	tyba 12/31/00	−518	−9,291	−9,927

2004	2005	2006	2007	2008	2009	2010	2011	2001–2006	2001–2011
–40,336	–40,201	–40,203	–40,065	–43,422	–45,359	–46,034	–13,871	–232,570	–421,321
–29,049	–32,774	–50,924	–59,378	–60,401	–61,652	–63,033	–19,035	–157,107	–420,606
—	—	–1,265	–2,566	–4,003	–5,414	–7,168	–4,456	–1,265	–24,872
—	—	–473	–955	–1.382	–1,793	–2,216	–1,323	–473	–8,140
–69,385	–72,975	–92,865	–102,964	–109,208	–114,218	–118,451	–38,685	–391,415	–874,939
–10,602	–12,786	–18,320	–19,000	–19,408	–20,532	–25,200	–26,197	–61,444	–171,782

PROVISION	EFFECTIVE	2001	2002	2003
Marriage Penalty Relief Provisions (Sunset 12/31/10)				
1. Standard deduction set at 2 times single for married filing jointly, phased in over 5 years	tyba 12/31/04	—	—	—
2. 15% rate bracket set at 2 times single for married filing jointly, phased in over 4 years	tyba 12/31/04	—	—	—
3. EIC Modification and Simplification—increase in joint returns beginning and ending income level for phaseout by $1,000 in 2002 through 2004, $2,000 in 2005 through 2007, and $3,000 in 2008, and indeed thereafter; simplify definition of earned income; use AGI instead of modified AGI; conform definition of qualifying child and tie breaker rules to those in Joint Committee on Taxation (JCT) simplification study; and allow math error procedure with federal case registry data beginning 2004[2]	tyba 12/31/01	—	−8	−847
Total of Marriage Penalty Relief Provisions (Sunset 12/31/10)		—	−8	−847
Education Provisions (Sunset 12/31/10)				
1. Education IRAs—Increase the annual contribution limit to $2,000; allow Education IRA contributions for special needs beneficiaries above the age of 18; allow corporations and other entities to contribute to Education IRAs; allow contributions until April 15 of the following year; allow a taxpayer to exclude Education IRA distributions from gross income and claim the Hope or Lifetime Learning credits as long as they are not used for the same expenses; repeal excise tax on contributions made to education IRA when contribution made by anyone on behalf of same beneficiary to QTP; modify phaseout range for married taxpayers;				

2004	2005	2006	2007	2008	2009	2010	2011	2001–2006	2001–2011
—	–685	–1,954	–2,580	–2,772	–3,164	–2,932	–831	–2,639	–14,918
—	–4208	–6,204	–6,559	–5,876	–4,737	–4,001	–1,150	–10,412	–32,734
–1,277	–1,243	–1,817	–1,819	–1,787	–2,258	–2,240	–2,348	–5,191	–15,643
–1,277	–6,136	–9,957	–10,958	–10,435	–10,159	–9,173	–4,329	–18,242	–63,295

PROVISION	EFFECTIVE	2001	2002	2003
allow tax-free expenditures for elementary and secondary school expenses; expand the definition of qualified expenses to include certain computers and related items	tyba 12/31/01	—	–203	–365
2. Qualified Tuition Plans—Tax-free distributions from state plans; allow private institutions to offer prepaid tuition plans, tax-deferred in 2002, with tax-free distributions beginning in 2004; allow a taxpayer to exclude QTP distributions from gross income and claim the Hope or Lifetime Learning credits as long as they are not used for the same expenses; expand definition of family member to include cousins; allow tax-free distributions for actual living expenses; ease rollover limitations; clarify coordination with the deduction for higher education expenses	tyba 12/31/01	—	–24	–53
3. Employer-Provided Assistance— Permanently extend the exclusion for undergraduate courses and graduate-level courses	cba 12/31/01	—	–519	–720
4. Student Loan Interest—Eliminate the 60-month rule; increase phaseout ranges to $50,000–$65,000 single/$100,000–$130,000 joint; indexed for inflation after 2002	ipa 12/31/01	—	–170	–245
5. Eliminate the tax on awards under the National Health Services Corps Scholarship program and F. Edward Hebert Armed Forces Health Professions Scholarship program	tyba 12/31/01	—	–1	–1
6. Increase arbitrage rebate exception for governmental bonds used to finance qualified school construction from $10 million to $15 million[3]	bia 12/31/01	—	3	–3
7. Issuance of tax-exempt private activity bonds for qualified education facilities				

2004	2005	2006	2007	2008	2009	2010	2011	2001–2006	2001–2011
–461	–561	–667	–778	–892	–1,013	–1,136	–295	–2,256	–6,370
–81	–111	–141	–170	–200	–234	–256	–64	–410	–1,334
–760	–804	–852	–904	–958	–1,012	–1,068	–267	–3,656	–7,865
–262	–277	–289	–305	–321	–338	–356	–89	–1,243	–2,651
–1	–1	–1	–1	–1	–1	–1	[3]	–4	–8
–5	–6	–11	–15	–16	–17	–18	–19	–25	–109

PROVISION	EFFECTIVE	2001	2002	2003
with annual state volume caps the greater of $10 per resident or $5 million	bia 12/31/01	—	–5	–19
8. Above-the-line deduction for qualified higher education expenses in 2002 through 2005	tyba 12/31/01	—	–1,535	–2,063
Total of Education Provisions (Sunset 12/31/10)		—	–2,457	–3,469

Estate and Gift Provisions
(Sunset 12/31/10)

1. Phase in Repeal of Estate and Generation-Skipping Transfer Taxes— Beginning in 2002, repeal the 5% "bubble" (which phases out the lower rates) and repeal rates in excess of 50%; In 2003, repeal rates in excess of 49%, in 2004 in excess of 48%, in 2005 in excess of 47%, in 2006 in excess of 46%, and in 2007 through 2009 in excess of 45%; reduce state death tax credit rates by 25% in 2002, 50% in 2003, 75% in 2004, and repeal in 2005; Increase the unified credit to $1 million in 2002 and 2003, $1.5 million in 2004 and 2005, $2 million in 2006 through 2008, and $3.5 million in 2009; repeal section 2057 in 2004; repeal estate and generation-skipping transfer taxes in 2010; retain gift tax in 2010 and thereafter with $1 million lifetime gift exclusion and gift tax rates set at the highest individual income tax rate; carryover basis applies to transfers at death after 12/31/09 of assets fully owned by decedents, except: (1) $1.3 million of additional basis and certain loss carryforwards of the decedent are allowed to be added to carryover basis, and (2) an additional $3 million of basis is allowed to be added to carryover basis of assets going to surviving spouse; certain reporting requirements on bequests	dda & gma 12/31/01	—	—	–6,383

2004	2005	2006	2007	2008	2009	2010	2011	2001–2006	2001–2011
–38	–61	–88	–120	–155	–191	–227	–251	–212	–1,156
–2,683	–2,911	–730	—	—	—	—	—	–9,921	–9,921
–4,291	–4,732	–2,779	–2,293	–2,543	–2,806	–3,062		–985 –17,727	–29,414
–5,031	–7,054	–4,051	–9,695	–11,862	–12,701	–23,036	–53,422	–22,519	–133,235

PROVISION	EFFECTIVE	2001	2002	2003
2. Expand Availability of Estate Tax Exclusion for Conservation Easements— Repeal the 25-mile and 10-mile limits, and clarify the date for determining easement compliance	dda 12/31/00	—	−3	−19
3. Modifications to Generation-Skipping Transfer Tax Rules				
a. Deemed allocation of the generation-skipping transfer tax exemption to lifetime transfers to trusts that are not direct skips	ta 12/31/00	—	−1	−3
b. Retroactive allocation of the generation-skipping tax exemption ..	generally 12/31/00	—	−1	−4
c. Severing of trusts holding property having an inclusion ratio of greater than zero	—			
d. Modification of certain valuation rules	—			
e. Relief from late elections	—			
f. Substantial compliance	—			
4. Expand Availability of Installment Payment Relief Under Section 6166 to:				
a. increase from 15 to 45 the number of partners of a partnership or shareholders in a corporation eligible for installment payments of estate tax under Section 6166	dda 12/31/01	—	—	−285
b. Qualified lending and finance business interests	dda 12/31/01	—	—	−103
c. Certain holding company stock	dda 12/31/01	—	—	−171
5. Waiver of statue of limitations for refunds of recapture of estate tax under Section 2032A	DOE	—	−100	−25
Total of Estate and Gift Provisions (Sunset 12/31/10)		—	−105	−6,993

2004	2005	2006	2007	2008	2009	2010	2011	2001–2006	2001–2011
−28	−29	−30	−32	−34	−36	−39	−42	−10	−292
−4	−4	−4	−4	−4	−4	−4	−4	−16	−36
−6	−6	−6	−6	−6	−6	−6	−6	−23	−53
				-Included in Item 3.b.-					
				Included in Item 3.b.-					
				Included in Item 3.b.-					
				Included in Item 3.b.-					
−297	−330	−364	−394	−383	−381	−371	−358	−1,276	−3,163
−84	−64	−43	−21	−22	−24	−25	−27	−295	−413
−140	−107	−72	−34	−47	−49	−42	−45	−491	−688
—	—	—	—	—	—	—	—	−125	−125
−5,590	−7,594	−4,570	−10,186	−12,358	−13,201	−23,523	−53,904	−24,854	−138,005

PROVISION	EFFECTIVE	2001	2002	2003
Pension and IRA Provisions (Generally Sunset 12/31/10)				
Individual Retirement Arrangement Provisions				
1. Modification of IRA Contribution Limits—Increase the maximum contribution limit for traditional and Roth IRAs to: $3,000 in 2002 through 2004, $4,000 in 2005 through 2007, and $5,000 in 2008; index in years thereafter............	tyba 12/31/01	—	−368	−847
2. IRA Catch-up Contributions—Increase maximum contribution limits for traditional and Roth IRAs for individuals age 50 and above by $500 in 2002 and $1,000 in 2006	tyba 12/31/01	—	−69	−151
3. Deemed IRAs under employee plans	pyba 12/31/02			
Total of Individual Retirement Arrangement Provisions		—	−437	−998
Provisions for Expanding Coverage				
1. Increase contribution and benefit limits:				
a. Increase limitation on exclusion for elective deferrals to: $11,000 in 2002, $12,000 in 2003, $13,000 in 2004, $14,000 in 2005, and $15,000 in 2006; index thereafter[4,5]............	yba 12/31/01	—	—	−100
b. Increase limitation on SIMPLE elective contributions to: $7,000 in 2002, $8,000 in 2003, $9,000 in 2004, and $10,000 in 2005; index thereafter[4,5]	yba 12/31/01	—	−10	−30
c. Increase defined benefit dollar limit to $160,000..............................	yba 12/31/01	—	−23	−42
d. Lower early retirement age to 62; lower normal retirement age to 65 ...	yba 12/31/01	—	−3	−4
e. Increase annual addition limitation for defined contribution plans to				

2004	2005	2006	2007	2008	2009	2010	2011	2001–2006	2001–2011
−1,054	−1,693	−2,346	−2,582	−3,148	−3,817	−4,243	−3,033	−6,308	−23,132
−174	−176	−225	−293	−252	−211	−234	−182	−795	−1,968
				Negligible Revenue Effect					
−1,228	−1,869	−2,571	−2,875	−3,400	−4,028	−4,477	−3,215	−7,103	−25,100
−328	−500	−636	−708	−753	−797	−880	−436	−1,564	−5,138
−42	−51	−55	−59	−63	−66	−69	−35	−188	−480
−46	−47	−48	−49	−54	−57	−56	−8	−207	−432
−4	−5	−5	−5	−5	−5	−5	−2	−21	−43

PROVISION	EFFECTIVE	2001	2002	2003
$40,000 with indexing in $1,000 increments [4]	yba 12/31/01	—	–7	–15
f. Increase qualified plan compensation limit to $200,000 with indexing in $5,000 increments[4] and expand availability of qualified plans to self-employed individuals who are exempt from the self-employment tax by reason of their religious beliefs	yba 12/31/01 & tyba 12/31/01	—	–55	–119
g. Increase limits on deferrals under deferred compensation plans of state and local governments and tax-exempt organizations to: $11,000 in 2002, $12,000 in 2003, $13,000 in 2004, $14,000 in 2005, and $15,000 in 2006; Index thereafter [4,5]	yba 12/31/0l	—	–29	–61
2. Plan loans for S corporation owners, partners, and sole proprietors	yba 12/31/01	—	–21	–32
3. Modification of top-heavy rules	yba 12/31/01	—	–4	–8
4. Elective deferrals not taken into account for purposes of deduction limits	yba 12/31/0l	—	–47	–88
5. Repeal of coordination requirements for deferred compensation plans of state and local governments and tax-exempt organizations[4]	yba 12/31/01	—	–16	–27
6. Elimination of user fee for certain requests regarding small employer pension plans with at least one non-highly compensated employee[6]	rma 12/31/01	—	–7	–10
7. Definition of compensation for purposes of deduction limits[4]	yba 12/31/01	—	–1	–3
8. Increase stock bonus and profit sharing plan deduction limit from 15% to 25%[4]	tyba 12/31/01	—	–7	–14
9. Option to treat elective deferrals as after-tax Roth contributions	yba 12/31/05	—	—	—

2004	2005	2006	2007	2008	2009	2010	2011	2001–2006	2001–2011
−19	−21	−17	−17	−20	−23	−27	−14	−79	−180
−125	−143	−141	−157	−154	−170	−184	−98	−583	−1,346
−87	−108	−127	−138	−147	−155	−164	−84	−411	−1,098
−34	−36	−39	−41	−44	−47	−49	−19	−162	−362
−10	−11	−13	−14	−16	−17	−19	−10	−45	−121
−103	−111	−119	−127	−135	−144	−152	−103	−468	−1,129
−27	−25	−23	−24	−24	−24	-24	−14	−118	−228
—	—	—	—	—	—	—	—	−17	−17
−3	−3	−3	−4	−4	−4	−4	−2	−14	−31
−16	−18	−19	−21	−23	−24	−26	−14	−75	−182
—	—	185	236	172	90	−5	−358	185	320

PROVISION	EFFECTIVE	2001	2002	2003
10. Nonrefundable credit to certain individuals for elective deferrals and IRA contributions (sunset 12/31/06)	tyba 12/31/01	—	−1,036	−2,096
11. Small business (100 or fewer employees) tax credit for new retirement plan expenses—first 3 years of the plan	7	—	−3	−12
12. Treatment of nonresident aliens engaged in international transportation services..	tyba 12/31/01	—	−2	−7
Total of Provisions for Expanding Coverage		—	−1,271	−12,668
Provisions for Enhancing Fairness for Women				
1. Additional catch-up contributions for individuals age 50 and above—increase the otherwise applicable contribution limit for all plans other than SIMPLE by $1,000 in 2002, $2,000 in 2003, $3,000 in 2004, $4,000 in 2005, and $5,000 in 2006 and thereafter; index in $500 increments after 2006; SIMPLE plan catch-ups would be 50% of that applicable to other plans (nondiscrimination rules would not apply)[4]	tyba 12/31/01	—	−124	−243
2. Equitable treatment for contributions of employees to defined contribution plans[4]	yba 12/31/01	—	−45	−84
3. Faster vesting of certain employer matching contributions........................	cf pyba 12/31/01			
4. Simplify and update the minimum distribution rules by modifying postdeath distribution rules	yba 12/31/01	—	3	−1
5. Clarification of tax treatment of division of section 457 plan benefits upon divorce	tdapma 12/31/01			
6. Modification of safe harbor relief for				

2004	2005	2006	2007	2008	2009	2010	2011	2001–2006	2001–2011
−1,963	−1,856	−1,746	−920	−102	−91	−89	−86	−8,698	−9,987
−21	−29	−29	−29	−27	−26	−25	−22	−94	−223
−7	−7	−8	−8	−8	−8	−8	−5	−31	−68
−2,835	−2,971	−2,843	−2,085	−1,407	−1,568	−1,786	−1,310	−12,590	−20,745
−234	−164	−100	−84	−76	−63	−57	−38	−865	−1,184
−98	−106	−113	−121	−129	−138	−144	−75	−446	1,051
----------------------- *Negligible Revenue Effect* -----------------------									
−1	−2	−2	−2	−2	−2	−3	−3	−6	−18
----------------------- *Negligible Revenue Effect* -----------------------									

PROVISION	EFFECTIVE	2001	2002	2003
hardship withdrawals from 401(k) plans	yba 12/31/0l			
7. Waiver of tax on nondeductible contributions for domestic or similar workers	tyba 12/31/0l	—	3	3
Total of Provisions for Enhancing Fairness for Women		—	−169	−328
Provisions for Increasing Portability for Participants				
1. Rollovers allowed among governmental section 457 plans, section 403(b) plans, and qualified plans	da 12/31/01	—	27	−4
2. Rollovers of IRAs to workplace retirement plans	da 12/31/01			
3. Rollovers of after-tax retirement plan contributions....................................	dma 12/31/0l			
4. Waiver of 60-day rule	da 12/31/01			
5. Treatment of forms of qualified plan distributions	yba 12/31/01			
6. Rationalization of restrictions on distributions	da 12/31/01			
7. Purchase of service credit in governmental defined benefit plans	ta 12/31/0l			
8. Employers may disregard rollovers for cash-out amounts	da 12/31/01			
9. Minimum distribution and inclusion requirements for Section 457 plans.........	da 12/31/01			
Total of Provisions for Increasing Portability for Participants		—	27	−4
Provisions for Strengthening Pension Security and Enforcement				
1. Phase in repeal of 160% of current liability funding limit; extend maximum deduction rule	pyba 12/31/01	—	−14	−20

2004	2005	2006	2007	2008	2009	2010	2011	2001–2006	2001–2011
- Negligible Revenue Effect -									
–1	–2	–4	–6	–8	–10	–12	–14	–8	–57
–334	–274	–219	–213	–215	–211	–216	–130	1,325	–2,310
–4	–5	–5	–5	–6	–6	7	–43	10	–57
- Negligible Revenue Effect -									
- Negligible Revenue Effect -									
- Negligible Revenue Effect -									
- Negligible Revenue Effect -									
- Negligible Revenue Effect -									
- Negligible Revenue Effect -									
- Negligible Revenue Effect -									
- Considered in Other Provisions -									
–4	–5	–5	–5	–6	–6	–7	–43	10	–57
–36	–36	–38	–38	–39	–41	–42	–22	–144	–326

PROVISION	EFFECTIVE	2001	2002	2003
2. Excise tax relief for sound pension funding	yba 12/31/01	—	–2	–3
3. Notice of significant reduction in plan benefit accruals	pateo/a DOE			
4. Repeal 100% of compensation limit for multiemployer plans...........................	yba 12/31/01	—	–2	–4
5. Modification of section 415 aggregation rules for multiemployer plans	tyba 12/31/01	—	–1	–1
6. Investment of employee contributions in 401(k) plans	aiii TRA '97			
7. Prohibited allocations of stock in an ESOP $ corporation[8]	[8]	—	3	5
8. Automatic rollovers of certain mandatory distributions	dma frap	—	—	—
9. Clarification of treatment of contributions to multiemployer plans.......	yea DOE	—	—	–11
Total of Provisions for Strengthening Pension Security and Enforcement		—	–16	–34
Provisions for Reducing Regulatory Burdens				
1. Modification of timing of plan valuations	pyba 12/31/0I			
2. ESOP dividends may be reinvested without loss of dividend deduction	tyba 12/31/0I	—	–20	–49
3. Repeal transition rule relating to certain highly compensated employees	pyba 12/31/0I	—	–2	–3
4. Employees of tax-exempt entities[9]	DOE			
5. Treatment of employer-provided retirement advice	yba 12/31/01			
6. Repeal of multiple use test	yba 12/31/01			
Total of Provisions for Reducing Regulatory Burdens		—	–22	–52

2004	2005	2006	2007	2008	2009	2010	2011	2001–2006	2001–2011
–3	–3	–3	–3	–3	–3	–3	–3	–14	–29
- Negligible Revenue Effect -
–4	–4	–4	–5	–5	–5	–5	–3	–18	–41
–1	–1	–1	–1	–1	–1	–1	–1	–4	–8
- Negligible Revenue Effect -
6	8	8	9	10	10	10	11	30	81
–7	–29	–30	–32	–33	–33	–34	–26	–66	–224
–19	–32	–38	–35	–30	–26	–19	–14	–100	–224
–64	–97	–106	–105	–101	–99	–94	–58	–316	–771
- Negligible Revenue Effect -
–59	–63	–66	–69	–71	–74	–77	–39	–259	–588
–3	–3	–3	–4	–4	–4	–4	–2	–14	–32
- Negligible Revenue Effect -
- Negligible Revenue Effect -
- Considered in Other Provisions -
–62	–66	–69	–73	–75	–78	–81	–41	–272	–620

PROVISION	EFFECTIVE	2001	2002	2003
Miscellaneous Provision—Allow electing Alaska Native Settlement Trusts to tax income to the trust not the beneficiaries[11] .... [12]		—	–4	–4
Total of Pension and IRA Provisions (Generally Sunset 12/31/10)		—	–1,892	–4,088
AMT Relief—Increase Exemption by $2,000 (Single) and $4,000 (Joint) in 2001 through 2004 (Sunset 12/31/04)	tyba 12/31/00	–178	–2,311	–3,161
Modification to Corporate Estimated Tax Requirements; Special Estimated Tax Rules for Certain 2001 and 2004 Corporate Estimated Tax Payments	DOE	–32,921	32,921	—
Expansion of Authority to Postpone Certain Tax Deadlines Due to Disaster (Sunset 12/31/10)	doa DOE		[3]	[13]
Miscellaneous Provisions (Generally Sunset 12/31/10)				
1. Adoption credit—increase the expense limit and the exclusion to $10,000 for both non-special needs and special needs adoptions, and beginning in 2003, make the credit independent of expenses for special needs adoptions, permanently extend the credit and the exclusion, increase the phaseout start point to $150,000, index for inflation the expenses limit and the phaseout start point for both the credit and the exclusion, and allow the credit to apply to the AMT	generally tyba 12/31/01	—	–51	–191
2. Provide an employer-provided child care credit of 25% for child care expenditures and 10% for child care resource and referral expenditures..........	tyba 12/31/01	—	–48	–108
3. Exclude from gross income certain payments made to Holocaust survivors or their heirs	aro/a 1/1/00	—	—	–3

2004	2005	2006	2007	2008	2009	2010	2011	2001–2006	2001–2011
–3	–3	–3	–3	–3	–4	–4	–1	–17	–33
–4,530	–5,285	–5,816	–5,259	–5,207	–5,994	–6,665	–4,798	–21,613	–49,636
–4,605	–3,646	—	—	—	—	—	—	–13,901	–13,901
–6,606	–6,606	—	—	—	—	—	—	—	—
13	13	13	13	13	13	13	13	13	14
–252	–293	–325	–349	–375	–403	–432	–464	–1,112	–3,135
–129	–142	–156	–169	–178	–188	–196	–90	–584	–1,405
–3	–3	–3	–3	–3	–3	–3	–3	–14	–31

PROVISION	EFFECTIVE	2001	2002	2003
4. Dependent care tax credit—Increase the credit rate to 35%, increase the eligible expenses to $3,000 for one child and $6,000 for two or more children (not indexed), and increase the start of the phaseout to $15,000 of AGI	tyba 12/31/02	—	—	−336
Total of Miscellaneous Provisions (Generally Sunset 12/31/10)		—	−99	−638
Net Total[15,16].....................................		−73,808	−37,763	−90,602

Note: Details may not add to totals due to rounding.
Legend for "Effective" column:
aiii TRA'97 = as if included in the Taxpayer Relief Act of 1997
aro/a = amounts received on or after
bia = bonds issued after
cba = courses beginning after
cf = contributions for

da = distributions after
dda = decedents dying after
dma = distributions made after
doa = disasters occurring after
DOE = date of enactment
frap = Federal regulations are prescribed
gma = gifts made after

1. The estimates presented in this table include the effects of certain behavioral responses to the tax proposals, including shifts between nontaxable and taxable sources of income, changes in amounts of charitable giving, and changes in the timing of realization of some sources of income. While the estimates do not include the effects of these proposals on economic growth, the proposals are likely to result in modest increases in growth of the economy during the 10-year budget estimating period. The largest component of the proposals, the marginal rate cuts, will provide incentives for more work, investment, and savings.
2. Estimate assumes that any constitutional challenge based on the use of federal case registry data would not be successful.
3. Loss of less than $500,000.
4. Provision includes interaction with other provisions in Provisions for Expanding Coverage.
5. Provision includes interaction with the Individual Retirement Arrangement Provisions.
6. Estimate provided by the Congressional Budget Office.
7. Effective for costs paid or incurred in taxable years beginning after December 31, 2001, with respect to qualified employer plans established after such date.
8. Generally effective with respect to years beginning after December 31, 2004. In the case of an ESOP established after March 14, 2001, or an ESOP established on or before such date if the employer maintaining the plan was not an S corporation on such date, the proposal would be effective with respect to plan years ending after March 14, 2001.
9. Directs the Secretary of the Treasury to modify rules through regulations.
10. Effective for distributions from terminating plans that occur after the PBGC has adopted final regulations implementing provision.
11. Special federal income tax rules would apply if the trust makes an election for its first taxable year ending after the date of enactment.
12. Effective for taxable years of electing Settlement Trusts ending after the date of enactment, and to contributions made to such trust made after the date of enactment.

2004	2005	2006	2007	2008	2009	2010	2011	2001–2006	2001–2011
432	–413	–393	–380	–352	–317	–296	–73	–1,573	–2,991
–816	–851	–877	–901	–908	–911	–927	–630	–3,283	–7,562
–107,702	–107,399	–135,202	–151,661	–160,067	–167,821	–187,001	–129,528	–552,480	–1,348,537

iafpbnet = interest accruing for periods beginning not earlier than
ipa = interest paid after
noitta = notice of intent to terminate after
pateo/a = plan amendments taking effect on or after
pea = plans established after
pyba = plan years beginning after

rma = requests made after
ta = transfers after
tdapma = transfers, distributions, and payments made after
tyba = taxable years beginning after
yba = years beginning after
yea = years ending after

13. Loss of less than $1 million.
14. Loss of less than $5 million.
15. Includes the following effect on fiscal year outlays (millions)

2001	2002	2003	2004	2005	2006	2007	2008	2009	2010	2011	2001–2006	2001–1011
—	6,226	6,660	7,006	7,081	9,597	1,542	9,360	9,668	11,080	12,244	36,510	88,404

16. Taxpayers affected by the AMT: present law (millions of taxpayers)

2001	2002	2003	2004	2005	2006	2007	2008	2009	2010	2011
1.5	3.5	4.3	5.6	7.1	8.7	10.5	12.8	14.9	17.5	20.7

Taxpayers affected by the AMT: proposal (millions of taxpayers)

| 1.4 | 2.7 | 3.3 | 5.3 | 13.0 | 19.6 | 23.9 | 29.1 | 32.1 | 35.5 | 20.7 |

Source: Joint Committee on Taxation.

Glossary

accelerated cost recovery system (ACRS) A statutory method of depreciation allowing accelerated rates for most types of property used in business and income-producing activities during the years 1981 through 1986. It has been superseded by the modified accelerated cost recovery system (MACRS) for assets placed in service after 1986.

accelerated depreciation Depreciation method that allows faster write-offs than straight-line rates in the earlier periods of the useful life of an asset. For example, in the first few years of recovery, MACRS allows a 200 percent double declining balance write-off, twice the straight-line rate.

accountable reimbursement plan An employer reimbursement or allowance arrangement that requires you to adequately substantiate business expenses to your employer, and to return any excess reimbursement.

accrual method of accounting A business method of accounting requiring income to be reported when earned and expenses to be deducted when incurred. However, deductions generally may not be claimed until economic performance has occurred.

acquisition debt Debt used to buy, build, or construct a principal residence or second home and that generally qualifies for a full interest expense deduction.

active participation Test for determining deductibility of IRA deductions. Active participants in employer retirement plans are subject to IRA deduction phaseout rules if adjusted gross income exceeds certain thresholds.

adjusted basis A statutory term describing the cost used to determine your profit or loss from a sale or exchange of property. It is generally your original cost, increased by capital improvements and decreased by depreciation, depletion, and other capital write-offs.

adjusted gross income (AGI) Important tax term representing gross income less allowable adjustments, such as IRA, alimony, and Keogh deductions. AGI determines whether various tax benefits are phased out, such as personal exemptions, itemized deductions, and the rental loss allowance.

alimony Payments made to a separated or divorced spouse as required by a decree or agreement. Qualifying payments are deductible by the payer and taxable to the payee.

alternative minimum tax (AMT) A tax triggered if certain tax benefits reduce your regular income tax below the tax computed on Form 6251 for AMT purposes.

amended return On Form 1040X, you may file an amended return within a three-year period to correct a mistake made on an original or previously amended return.

amortization of intangibles Writing off an investment in intangible assets over the projected life of the assets.

amount realized A statutory term used to figure your profit or loss on a sale or exchange. Generally, it is sales proceeds plus mortgages assumed or taken subject to, less transaction expenses, such as commissions and legal costs.

amount recognized The amount of gain reportable and subject to tax. On certain tax-free exchanges of property, gain is not recognized in the year it is realized.

annualized rate A rate for a period of less than a year computed as though for a full year.

annuity An annual payment of money by a company or an individual to a person called the annuitant. Payment is for a fixed period or the life of the annuitant. Tax consequences depend on the type of contract and funding.

applicable federal rate   Interest rate fixed by the Treasury for determining imputed interest.

appreciation in value   Increase in value of property due to market conditions. When you sell appreciated property, you pay tax on the appreciation since the date of purchase. When you donate appreciated property held for the long term, you may generally deduct the appreciated value.

assessment   With regard to the Internal Revenue Service, the IRS action of fixing tax liability that sets in motion collection procedures, such as charging interest, imposing penalties, and, if necessary, seizing property.

asset   Anything owned that has cash or exchange value.

assignment   The legal transfer of property, rights, or interest to another person called an assignee. You cannot avoid tax on income by assigning the income to another person.

at-risk rules   Rules limiting loss deductions to cash investments and personal liability notes. An exception for real estate treats certain nonrecourse commercial loans as amounts "at risk."

attorneys' fee awards   Taxpayers who prevail in the Tax Court or other federal court may recover up to a certain amount for attorneys' fees, plus other litigation expenses, by showing that the IRS position was unreasonable.

audit   An IRS examination of your tax return, generally limited to a three-year period after you file.

averaging Some retirees may use favorable averaging methods to compute tax on lump-sum distributions if they were born before 1936.

away from home A tax requirement for deducting travel expenses on a business trip. Sleeping arrangements are required for at least one night before returning home.

B

balloon A final payment on a loan in one lump sum.

basis Generally, the amount paid for property. You need to know your basis to figure gain or loss on a sale.

boot Generally, the receipt of cash or its equivalent accompanying an exchange of property. In a tax-free exchange, boot is subject to immediate tax.

C

calendar year A year that ends on December 31.

cancellation of debt Release of a debt without consideration by a creditor. Cancellations of debt are generally taxable.

capital The excess of assets over liabilities.

capital asset Property subject to capital gain or loss treatment. Almost all assets you own are considered capital assets except for certain business assets or works you created.

capital expenses Costs that are not currently deductible and that are added to the basis of property. A capital expense generally increases the value of property. When added to depreciable property, the cost is deductible over the life of the asset.

capital gain distribution A mutual-fund distribution allocated to gains realized on the sale of fund portfolio assets. You report the distribution as long-term capital gain even if you held the fund shares for the short term.

capital gain or loss The difference between amount realized and adjusted basis on the sale or exchange of capital assets. Long-term capital gains are taxed favorably. Capital losses are deducted first against capital gains, and then again up to $3,000 of other income.

capital loss carryover A capital loss that is not deductible because it exceeds the annual $3,000 capital loss ceiling. A carryover loss may be deducted from capital gains of later years plus up to $3,000 of ordinary income.

capitalization Adding a cost or expense to the basis of the property.

carryback A tax technique for receiving a refund of back taxes by applying a deduction or credit from a current tax year to a prior tax year. For example, a business net operating loss incurred in 2001 may be carried back for two years.

carryforward A tax technique of applying a loss or credit from a current year to a later year. For example, a business net operating loss may be carried forward 20 years instead of being carried back for two years.

cash method of accounting   Reporting income when actually or constructively received and deducting expenses when paid. Certain businesses may not use the cash method.

casualty loss   Loss from an unforeseen and sudden event that is deductible, subject to a 10 percent income floor and $100 reduction for personal losses.

charitable contributions   An itemized deduction is allowed for donations to qualifying charities. For property donations, the deductible amount depends on the type of property and donee organization, your holding period, and in some cases how the property is used.

check the box   A term describing a classification rule that provides automatic partnership pass-through treatment for most businesses with two or more members unless the members elect on Form 8832 to be taxed as a corporation.

child and dependent care credit   A credit of up to 30 percent based on certain care expenses incurred to allow you to work.

child support   Payments to support a minor child generally made to a custodial parent under a divorce or separation decree or agreement. The payments are not deductible.

community income Income earned by persons domiciled in community property states and treated as belonging equally to husband and wife.

condemnation The seizure of property by a public authority for a public purpose. Tax on gain realized on many conversions may be deferred.

constructive receipt A tax rule that taxes income that is not received by you but that you may draw upon.

consumer interest Interest incurred on personal debt and consumer credit. Consumer interest is not deductible.

convention Rule for determining MACRS depreciation in the year property is placed in service. Either a half-year convention or mid-quarter convention applies.

corporation An entity organized under state law and generally treated as a separate taxpayer unless an S election is made.

credit A tax credit directly reduces tax liability, as opposed to a deduction that reduces income subject to tax.

D

declining balance method A rapid depreciation method determined by a constant percentage based on useful life and applied to the adjusted basis of the property.

deductions   Items directly reducing income. Personal deductions such as for mortgage interest, state and local taxes, and charitable contributions are allowed only if deductions are itemized on Schedule A, but deductions such as for alimony, capital losses, moving expenses to a new job location, business losses, student loan interest, and IRA and Keogh deductions are deducted from gross income even if itemized deductions are not claimed.

deferred compensation   A portion of earnings withheld by an employer or put into a retirement plan for distribution to the employee at a later date. If certain legal requirements are met, the deferred amount is not taxable until actually paid—for example, after retirement.

deficiency   The excess of the tax assessed by the IRS over the amount reported on your return.

defined benefit plan   A retirement plan that pays fixed benefits based on actuarial projections.

defined contribution plan   A retirement plan that pays benefits based on contributions to individual accounts, plus accumulated earnings. Contributions are generally based on a percentage of salary or earned income.

dependency exemption   A fixed deduction allowed to every taxpayer, except anyone who may be claimed as a dependent by another person. Extra exemption deductions are allowed for a spouse on a joint return and for each qualifying dependent.

dependent   A person supported by another person. If certain tests are met, a dependency exemption may be claimed for the dependent.

depletion   Deduction claimed for the use of mineral resources.

depreciable property   A business or income-producing asset with a useful life exceeding one year.

depreciation   Writing off the cost of depreciable property over a period of years, usually its class life or recovery period specified in the tax law.

depreciation recapture   An amount of gain on the sale of certain depreciable property that is treated as ordinary income in the case of personal property.

disaster losses   Casualty losses such as from a storm, in areas declared by the president to warrant federal assistance. An election may be made to deduct the loss in the year before the loss or in the year of the loss.

dividend   A distribution made by a corporation to its shareholders generally of company earnings or surplus.

E

earned income   Compensation for performing personal services. You must have earned income for a deductible IRA.

earned income credit A credit allowed to taxpayers with earned income or adjusted gross income (AGI) below certain thresholds.

education credits There are two education credits: the Hope credit and the Lifetime Learning credit.

Education IRA A special IRA account set up to fund education expenses of a student.

estate tax A tax imposed on the value of a decedent's taxable estate, after deductions and credits.

estimated tax Advance payment of current tax liability based either on wage withholdings or on installment payments of your estimated tax liability. To avoid penalties, you generally must pay to the IRS either 90 percent of your final tax liability, or either 100 percent or 110 percent of the prior year's tax liability, depending on your adjusted gross income.

exemption *See* **dependency exemption**.

F

fair market value What a willing buyer would pay to a willing seller when neither is under any compulsion to buy or sell.

fiduciary A person or corporation such as a trustee, executor, or guardian who manages property for another person.

first-year expensing In 2001, a deduction of up to $24,000 (or $44,000 for qualifying businesses in an enterprise zone) of the cost of business equipment in the year placed in service.

fiscal year A 12-month period ending on the last day of any month other than December. Partnerships, S corporations, and personal service corporations are limited in their choice of fiscal years and face special restrictions.

flexible spending arrangements A salary reduction plan that allows employees to pay for enhanced medical coverage or dependent care expenses on a tax-free basis.

foreign earned income exclusion In 2001, up to $78,000 of foreign earned income is exempt from tax if a foreign residence or physical presence test is met.

foreign tax credit A credit for income taxes paid to a foreign country or U.S. possession.

401(k) plan A deferred pay plan, authorized by Section 401(k) of the Internal Revenue Code, under which a percentage of an employee's salary is withheld and placed in a savings account or the company's profit-sharing plan. Income accumulates on the deferred amount until withdrawn by the employee at age $59\frac{1}{2}$ or when the employee retires or leaves the company.

G

gift tax   Gifts in excess of a $10,000 per donee annual exclusion are subject to gift tax, but the tax may be offset by a unified gift and estate tax credit.

grantor trust rules   Tax rules that tax the grantor of a trust on the trust income.

gross income   The total amount of income received from all sources before exclusions and deductions.

gross receipts   Total business receipts reported on Schedule C or Schedule C-EZ before deducting adjustments for returns and allowances and cost of goods sold.

group term life insurance   Employees are not taxed on up to $50,000 of group term coverage.

H

head of household   Generally, an unmarried person who maintains a household for dependents and is allowed to compute his or her tax based on head of household rates, which are more favorable than single person rates.

hobby loss   Hobby expenses are deductible only up to income from the activity; loss deductions are not allowed.

holding period   The length of time that an asset is owned and that generally determines long- or short-term capital gain treatment.

home equity debt   Debt secured by a principal residence or second home to the extent of the excess of fair market value over acquisition debt. An interest deduction is generally allowed for home equity debt up to $100,000 ($50,000 if married filing separately).

I

imputed interest   Interest deemed earned on seller-financed sales or low-interest loans, where the parties' stated interest rate is below the applicable IRS federal rate.

incentive stock option   Options meeting tax law tests that defer tax on the option transaction until the obtained stock is sold.

income in respect of a decedent   Income earned by a person before death but taxable to an estate or heir who receives it.

independent contractor   One who controls his or her own work and reports as a self-employed person.

individual retirement account (IRA)   A retirement account to which up to $2,000 may be contributed annually, but deductions for the contributions are restricted if you are covered by a company retirement plan. Earnings on IRA contributions accumulate tax free.

innocent spouse   A spouse who claims that he or she should not be liable on a joint return.

installment sale   A sale of property that allows for tax deferment if at least one payment is received after the end of the tax year in which the sale occurs. The installment method does not apply to year-end sales of publicly traded securities. Dealers may not use the installment method. Investors with very large installment balances could face a special tax.

intangible assets   Intangible assets that come within Section 197, such as goodwill, are amortizable over a 15-year period.

inter vivos or lifetime trust   A trust created during the lifetime of the person who created the trust. If irrevocable, income on the trust principal is generally shifted to the trust beneficiaries.

investment in the contract   The total cost investment in an annuity. When annuity payments are made, the portion allocable to the cost investment is tax free.

investment interest   Interest on debt used to carry investments, but not including interest expense from a passive activity. Deductions are limited to net investment income.

involuntary conversion   Forced disposition of property due to condemnation, theft, or casualty. Tax on gain from involuntary conversions may be deferred if replacement property is purchased.

itemized deductions   Items, such as interest, state and local taxes, charitable contributions, and medical deductions, claimed on Schedule A of Form 1040. Itemized deductions are subtracted from adjusted gross income to arrive at taxable income. The amount of itemized deductions is also subject to a reduction when adjusted gross income exceeds certain limits.

J

joint return   A return filed by a married couple reporting their combined income and deductions. Joint return status provides tax savings to many couples.

joint tenants   Ownership of property by two persons. When one dies, the decedent's interest passes to the survivor.

K

Keogh plan   Retirement plan set up by a self-employed person, providing tax-deductible contributions, tax-free income accumulations until withdrawal, and favorable averaging for qualifying lump-sum distributions.

kiddie tax   The tax on the investment income in excess of $1,500 (for 2001) of a dependent child under age 14, based on the parents' marginal tax rate and computed on Form 8615.

L

legally separated   A husband and wife who are required to live apart from each other by the terms of a decree of separate maintenance. Payments under the decree are deductible by the payer and taxable to the payee as alimony.

like-kind exchange   An exchange of similar assets used in a business or held for investment on which gain may be deferred.

lump-sum distribution   Payments within one tax year of the entire amount due to a participant in a qualified retirement plan because of retirement, separation from service, reaching age $59\frac{1}{2}$, death, or, in the case of a self-employed person, disability or reaching age $59\frac{1}{2}$. Qualifying lump sums may be directly rolled over tax free, or, in some cases, are eligible for current tax under a favorable averaging method.

M

marital deduction   An estate tax and gift tax deduction for assets passing to a spouse. It allows estate and gift transfers completely free of tax.

market discount   The difference between face value of a bond and lower market price, attributable to rising interest rates. On a sale, gain on the bond is generally taxed as ordinary income to the extent of the discount.

material participation tests Rules for determining whether a person is active in a business activity for passive activity rule purposes. Unless the tests are met, passive loss limits apply.

medical savings account (MSA) A type of medical plan combining high-deductible medical insurance protection with an IRA-type savings account fund to pay unreimbursed medical expenses.

miscellaneous itemized deductions Generally, itemized deductions for job and investment expenses subject to a 2 percent of adjusted gross income floor.

modified accelerated cost recovery system (MACRS) Depreciation methods applied to assets placed in service after 1986.

modified adjusted gross income (MAGI) This is generally adjusted gross income increased by certain items such as tax-free foreign earned income. MAGI usually is used to determine phaseouts of certain deductions and credits.

mortgage interest Fully deductible interest on up to two residences if acquisition debt secured by a home is $1 million or less, and home equity debt is $100,000 or less.

moving expenses Certain expenses of moving to a new job location are deductible if distance and time tests are met.

N

net operating loss   A business loss that exceeds current income may be carried back against income of prior years and carried forward as a deduction from future income until eliminated.

nonperiodic distributions   A 20 percent withholding rule applies to nonperiodic distributions, such as lump-sum distributions, paid directly to employees from an employer plan.

nonrecourse financing   Debt on which a person is not personally liable. In case of nonpayment, the creditor must foreclose on property securing the debt. At-risk rules generally bar losses where there is nonrecourse financing, but an exception applies to certain nonrecourse financing for real estate.

nonresident alien   A person who is not a United States citizen or a permanent resident. Tax is generally limited to income from U.S. sources.

O

ordinary and necessary   A statutory requirement for the deductibility of a business expense.

ordinary income   Income other than capital gains.

ordinary loss   A loss other than a capital loss.

original issue discount (OID)   The difference between the face value of a bond and its original issue price. OID is reported on an annual basis as interest income.

P

partnership   An unincorporated business or income-producing entity organized by two or more persons. A partnership is not subject to tax but passes through to the partners all income, deductions, and credits, according to the terms of the partnership agreement.

passive activity loss rules   Rules that limit the deduction of losses from passive activities to income from other passive activities. Passive activities include investment rental operations or businesses in which you do not materially participate.

patronage dividend   A taxable distribution made by a cooperative to its members or patrons.

pension   Payments to an employee from an employer-funded retirement plan for past services.

percentage depletion   A deduction method that applies a fixed percentage to the gross income generated by mineral property.

personal exemption   An automatic exemption given to a taxpayer unless he or she may be claimed as a dependent by another taxpayer. For 2001, the exemption amount is $2,900. Exemptions are phased out for certain high-income taxpayers.

personal interest Tax term for interest on personal loans and consumer purchases. Such interest is not deductible.

placed in service The time when a depreciable asset is ready to be used. The date fixes the beginning of the depreciation period.

points Charges to the homeowner at the time of the loan. A point is equal to 1 percent. Depending on the type of loan, points may be currently deductible or amortized over the life of the loan.

premature distributions Withdrawals before age $59\frac{1}{2}$ from qualified retirement plans are subject to penalties unless specific exceptions are met.

probate estate Property held in a decedent's name passing by will.

profit-sharing plan A defined contribution plan under which the amount contributed to the employees' accounts is based on a percentage of the employer's profits.

provisional income If your provisional income exceeds a base amount, part of your Social Security benefits may be subject to tax.

Q

qualified charitable organization A nonprofit philan-thropic organization that is approved by the U.S. Treasury to receive charitable contribution deductions.

qualified plan A retirement plan that meets tax law tests and allows for tax deferment and tax-free accumulation of income until benefits are withdrawn. Pension, profit-shar-ing, stock bonus, employee stock ownership, Keogh plans, and IRAs may be qualified plans.

qualified state tuition plan (QSTP) A state-sponsored college savings plan.

qualifying widow or widower A filing status entitling the taxpayer with dependents to use joint tax rates for up to two tax years after the death of a spouse.

R

real estate investment trust (REIT) An entity that in-vests primarily in real estate and mortgages and passes through income to investors.

real estate professional An individual who, because of his or her real estate activity, qualifies to deduct rental losses from nonpassive income.

real property   Land and the buildings on land. Buildings are depreciable.

recognized gain or loss   The amount of gain or loss to be reported on a tax return. Gain may not be recognized on certain exchanges of property.

recovery property   Tangible depreciable property placed in service after 1980 and before 1987 and depreciable under ACRS.

refundable tax credit   A credit that entitles you to a refund even if you owe no tax for the year.

residence interest   Term for deductible mortgage interest on a principal residence and a second home.

residential rental property   Real property in which 80 percent or more of the gross income is from dwelling units. Under MACRS, depreciation is claimed over 27.5 years under the straight-line method.

return of capital   A distribution of your investment that is not subject to tax unless the distribution exceeds your investment.

revocable trust   A trust that may be changed or terminated by its creator or another person. Such trusts do not provide an income tax savings to the creator.

rollover   A tax-free reinvestment of a distribution from a qualified retirement plan into an IRA or other qualified plan within 60 days.

Roth IRA   A nondeductible contributory IRA that allows for tax-free accumulation of income.

royalty income   Amounts received for the use of property such as mineral property, a book, a movie, or a patent.

S

S corporation   A corporation that elects S status in order to receive tax treatment similar to a partnership.

salvage value   The estimated value of an asset at the end of its useful life. Salvage value is ignored by ACRS and MACRS rules.

scholarships   Grants to degree candidates receive tax-free treatment if awarded after August 16, 1986, and used for tuition and course-related expenses, but not room and board.

Section 179 deduction   Expensing deduction, in 2001 up to $24,000, allowed for investments in depreciable business equipment in the year the property is placed in service. The deduction may be as high as $44,000 for qualifying businesses in an enterprise zone.

Section 457 plan   Deferred compensation plan set up by a state or local government, or tax-exempt organization, that allows tax-free deferrals of salary.

Section 1231 property   Depreciable property used in a trade or business and held for more than a year. All Section 1231 gains and losses are netted; a net gain is treated as capital gain, a net loss as an ordinary loss.

self-employed person   An individual who operates a business or profession as a proprietor or independent contractor and reports self-employment income on Schedule C.

self-employment tax   Tax paid by self-employed persons to finance Social Security coverage. In 2001, there are two rates: a 12.4 percent rate that applies to a taxable earnings base of $80,400 or less and a 2.9 percent rate on all net earnings.

separate return   Return filed by a married person who does not file a joint return. Filing separately may save taxes where each spouse has separate deductions, but certain tax benefits require a joint return.

short sale   Sale of borrowed securities made to freeze a paper profit or to gain from a declining market.

short tax year   A tax year of less than 12 months. May occur with the start-up of a business or change in accounting method.

short-term capital gain or loss Gain or loss on the sale or exchange of a capital asset held one year or less.

simplified employee pension plan (SEP) IRA-type plan set up by an employer, rather than the employee. Salary-reduction contributions may be allowed to plans of small employers.

single The filing status of an individual who is not married on December 31 of the year for which a return is filed.

standard deduction A fixed deduction allowed to taxpayers who do not itemize deductions. The amount depends on filing status, age, and whether one is blind.

standard mileage rate A fixed rate allowed by the IRS for business auto expenses in place of deducting actual expenses.

statutory employees Certain employees, such as full-time life insurance salespersons, who may report income and deductions on Schedule C rather than on Schedule A as miscellaneous itemized deductions.

stock dividend A distribution of additional shares of a corporation's stock to its shareholders.

stock option A right to buy stock at a fixed price.

straight-line method A method of depreciating the cost of a depreciable asset on a pro rata basis over its cost-recovery period.

T

tangible personal property Movable property, such as desks, computers, machinery, and autos, depreciable over a five-year or seven-year period.

taxable income Net income after claiming all deductions from gross income and adjusted gross income, such as IRA deductions, itemized deductions, or the standard deduction, and personal exemptions.

tax deferral Shifting income to a later year, such as where you defer taxable interest to the following year by purchasing a Treasury bill or savings certificate maturing after the end of the current year. Investments in qualified retirement plans provide tax deferral.

tax home The area of your principal place of business or employment. You must be away from your tax home on a business trip to deduct travel expenses.

tax identification number For an individual, his or her Social Security number; for businesses, fiduciaries, and other nonindividual taxpayers, the employer identification number.

tax preference items Items that may subject a taxpayer to the alternative minimum tax (AMT).

tax rate schedules Used by taxpayers with taxable incomes of $100,000 or more.

tax-sheltered annuity A type of retirement annuity offered to employees of charitable organizations and educational systems, generally funded by employee salary-reduction contributions.

tax tables Used by taxpayers with taxable incomes of less than $100,000 to look up their tax amounts.

tax year A period (generally 12 months) for reporting income and expenses.

tenancy by the entireties A joint tenancy in real property in the name of both husband and wife. On the death of one tenant, the survivor receives the entire interest.

tenants in common Two or more persons who have undivided ownership rights in property. Upon death of a tenant, his or her share passes to his or her estate, rather than to the surviving tenant(s).

testamentary trust A trust established under a will.

trust An arrangement under which one person transfers legal ownership of assets to another person or corporation (the trustee) for the benefit of one or more third persons (beneficiaries).

U

unrecaptured Section 1250 gain Long-term gain realized on the sale of depreciable realty attributed to depreciation deductions and subject to a 25 percent capital gain rate.

useful life For property not depreciated under ACRS or MACRS, the estimate of time in which a depreciable asset will be used.

V

vacation home The tax law limits the deduction for a vacation home, broadly defined as any dwelling unit used by the owner or the owner's relatives for more than a specified period.

W

wash sales Sales on which losses are disallowed because you recover your market position within a 61-day period.

withholding An amount taken from income as a prepayment of an individual's tax liability for the year. In the case of wages, the employer withholds part of every wage payment. Backup withholding from dividend or interest income is required if you do not provide the payer with a correct taxpayer identification number. Withholding on pensions and IRAs is automatic unless you elect to waive withholding.

Index

Above-the-line deductions, 71
Acquisition indebtedness, 112
Adjusted gross estate, 105
Adjusted gross income (AGI), 31,
    55–56, 116–118, 130
Adjusted taxable estate, 92
Adopted children, tax treatment of,
    54, 57–58
Adoption assistance, 55
Adoption credit, 8–9
Adoption tax benefits, 42–46
Alternative minimum tax
    (AMT):
    child tax credit and, 5
    defined, 2
    earned income credit and, 57
    exemption amounts, 6, 30, 36
    marriage penalty and, 59
    nonrefundable credit for IRA
        contributions, 130
    relief from, generally, 36–37
Alternative minimum tax income
    (AMTI), 36
Annual additions, defined, 122

Annuities, 121, 124. *See also* 403(b)
    annuities
Anticutback rules, 152

Back taxes, rebate checks and, 18
Basis of property:
    carryover rules, 95–97, 109–110
    defined, 103
    stepped-up, 15–16, 93–100, 105–106,
        109–110
Beneficiary, minimum distribution
    rules, 136–137. *See also specific
    types of plans*
Bonuses, 27
Breakeven income level, 56

Cafeteria plans, 55
Carryover basis rules, 95–97,
    109–110
Cash-out rules, 155, 173–174
Catch-up contributions:
    457 plans, 133, 137–138
    IRAs, 119–121
    pension plans, 131–135

C corporation shareholders, plan
  loans, 159
Charitable contributions, 27
Child care facilities, *see* Dependent
  care facilities
Children, tax benefits relating to:
  adoption tax benefits, 42–46
  child tax credit, 39–42
  dependent care tax credit, 46–49
  earned income credit, 54–58,
    57–58
Child support, rebate checks and,
  19
Child tax credit:
  calculation of, 40
  development of, 39–42
  increase in, 5–6, 41–42
  limitation percentage, 41–42
  qualification for, 40
  refundable, 41–42
Clergy, 55
Cliff deductions, 71
Closely held businesses, estate tax,
  104–107
College education deduction:
  distributions, 73
  eligibility for, 72, 79–80
  income limits and phaseout, 72
  overview, 15, 70–72
Community property, estate taxes and,
  97, 99
Conservation easements, 110–112
Cost-of-living adjustments, 122–124

Decedent, *see* Estate taxes
Deductions, generally:
  above-the-line, 71
  acceleration, 27
  college tuition, 15, 70–74
  deferral of, 32
  elective deferral contributions,
    163–164
  family-owned business, 16, 86
  itemized, *see* Itemized deductions
  student loan interest, 14–15
Deferred compensation plans:
  contribution limit, 137–139
  elective deferrals, 157
  employee contributions, 169

repeal of coordination requirements
  for state and local governments
  and tax-exempt organizations,
  165–166
Defined benefit plans:
  amendments to, 155
  benefit limits, 122
  contribution limits, 120–123
  distributions, treatment of, 154
  tax credit for new retirement plan
    expenses, 168
  top-heavy plans, 160–162
Defined contribution plans:
  benefit limits, 123
  contribution limits, 11–12, 121–123
  distributions, treatment of,
    151–153
  employee contributions, generally,
    169–170
  top-heavy plans, 160–162
De minimis effect, 151, 153–154
De minimis fringe benefit, 176
Dependency exemptions, education
  credits, 77
Dependent care:
  assistance, 55
  credit, expansion of, 7–8
  facilities, employer credit for, 8
Dependent care tax credit:
  calculation of, 46, 48
  eligibility for, 46–47
  exclusion, 48–49
  maximum, 46–47
Dependents:
  relationship test, 54–55, 57–58
  support test, 55
Determination date, defined, 160
Determination letter requests,
  166–167
Development rights, 112–113
Disabled children, 54
Disqualified income, 54
Distributions, *see specific types of
  plans*
Dividends, 54
Divorce, 457 plan benefits, 139–140
Domestic employees, 144–145
Domestic international sales
  corporation, 99

Early retirement subsidy, 153–154, 156
Earned income credit:
alternative minimum tax and, 59
calculation of, 55–56
earned income, defined, 55, 59
marriage penalty, 7, 53, 56–57
parameters, 56–57
phaseout range, 57–58
qualifying child, 54–55, 57–58
Economic Growth and Tax Relief
Reconciliation Act of 2001:
major provisions, overview of, 2–19
purpose of, 1
sunset of, 1–2, 21, 34, 61, 85, 115
Educational assistance plans (EAPs),
74–75, 79–80
Education IRAs:
contributions, 61–64, 78, 80
distributions, tax treatment of,
63–65, 73, 77–80
education credits and, 77–79
income limitations, 63–64
overview, 13–14, 62
qualified education expenses, 64–65
rollovers, 63
special needs children, 65–66
Education tax breaks:
college tuition deduction, 15, 70–74,
79–80
educational assistance plans (EAPs),
74–75, 79–80
education IRAs, 13–14, 61–66, 77–80
employer-provided assistance, 14
scholarships under National Health
Service Corps and Armed Forces
Health Professions programs,
82–83
Section 529 qualified tuition plans,
14, 61, 66–70, 73
student loan interest deduction,
14–15, 80–82
Effective date:
automatic rollover, mandatory
distributions, 150
elective deferrals, 175
vesting schedules, 135
Elective deferrals, *see specific plans*
defined, 124
employees age 50 or older, 131–132

hardship withdrawals and, 143–144
increase in, 10–11, 55
limitations, 124–125
nonrefundable credit, 128–130
as Roth contributions, 126–128
Eligible individual account plan,
defined, 174–175
Employee exclusion, special needs
adoptions, 8–9, 43–45
Employee Retirement Income Security
Act (ERISA), 121, 155, 174
Employee stock ownership plan
(ESOP), 152
Employer, considerations for:
adoption assistance, 8, 42–44
dependent care assistance, 48–49
dependent care facilities, credit for,
8
education assistance exclusion, 14
retirement plan start-up costs, credit
for, 12
Employer matching contributions:
top-heavy plans, 162–163
vesting schedule, 13, 134–136
Employer-provided retirement advice,
treatment of, 176–177
Employer retirement plans:
elective deferrals, 10–11
IRA contribution limits and, 9–10
nondiscrimination rules, 10, 128
qualified, start-up costs, 12
Employer-sponsored retirement plans:
IRA contributions and, 116–117
rollover distributions, 145–146
Estate planning, *see* Estate taxes
Estate taxes:
basis increase for assets, 96–99
basis of property acquired from
decedent, 92–96
closely held businesses, installment
payment for, 104–107
conservation easements, 110–114
death taxes, defined, 93
deduction for state death taxes paid,
91–92
family-owned business deduction,
repeal of, 16
generation-skipping tax, 89, 91, 113
gift tax, 86–87, 90–91

Estate taxes (*Continued*)
  inherited assets, stepped-up basis, 15–16, 93–94, 96–100, 109
  $1 million lifetime exclusion, 15–16
  overview, 15–16
  reporting requirements, 102–104
  sale of principal residence, 100–102
  state death tax, defined, 93
  state death tax credit, 16–17, 91–92
  transfer of property in satisfaction of pecuniary bequest, 109–110
  transfers to foreign trusts, foreign estates, and nonresidents who are not U.S. citizens, 107–109
  unified credit, 87–88
Excise tax, 144, 156
Executor:
  estate taxes, 16, 104–105
  reporting requirements, 102

Fair market value, 16, 92, 98, 103, 107–110
Families, tax relief provisions:
  adoption tax, 42–46
  alternative minimum tax (AMT), 59
  children, 39–42
  dependent care tax credit, 46–49
  earned income credit, 53–59
  15 percent tax bracket for married couples filing joint returns, 51–53
  marriage penalty relief, 49–59
  sale of principal residence, 60
Family-owned business, estate tax deduction, 16, 86
Federal Case Registry of Child Support Orders, 59
15 percent tax bracket, 4–5, 7, 23, 50–53
Financial hardship, 142–143
Foreign investment companies, 99
Foreign personal holding company, 99
Foster child, tax treatment of, 54, 58
457 plans:
  catch-up contributions, 133–134, 137–138, 165
  contributions, 12, 129
  deferred compensation, maximum annual deferral, 137–139

divorce, tax treatment of benefits, 139–140
elective deferrals, 131–132, 165–166, 170
inclusion requirements, 140–141
minimum distribution requirements, 136–137, 140–141
rollover distributions, 13, 146–147
separation from service, 170, 172
401(k) plans:
  catch-up contributions, 131
  contributions, 12, 121–123
  distributions, treatment of, 152
  elective deferrals, 10–11, 124–126, 129, 131–133, 157, 163–164, 170
  employee contributions, investment of, 174–175
  employer contributions, deduction limits, 163
  new retirement plan expenses, tax credit for, 168–169
  Roth contribution program, 126–128
  separation from service, 170–172
403(b) annuities:
  contributions, 12
  elective deferrals, 10–11, 55, 124–126, 129, 131–132, 157, 164–165, 170
  exclusion allowance, 170
  minimum distribution rules, 136–137
  rollover distributions, 13, 145–147
  Roth contribution program, 126
  separation from service, 170, 172
Fringe benefits:
  employer-provided, 176–177
  nontaxable, 55

Gain or loss, sale of property, 93–94, 100–102, 110
Generation-skipping transfer (GST) tax, 89, 91
Gifts, reporting requirements, 102–104
Gift tax:
  $1 million lifetime exclusion, 15–16
  qualified tuition plans and, 67
  tax rates, 86–87

Grandchildren:
  gifts to, 113
  tax treatment of, 54, 57–58, *see*
    Generation-skipping transfer
    (GST) tax

Hardship withdrawals, pension plans,
  142–144
Head of household:
  alternative minimum tax (AMT)
    exemption, 6
  IRA contributions, 129
  personal exemption, 34
  rebate check, 3, 29
  tax rate reductions, 5, 22
  tax rate schedules for 2001, 25
  10 percent bracket income levels, 23
Highly compensated individuals:
  defined contribution plan, 11–12
  elective deferrals, 10, 133
  fringe benefits, employer-provided,
    177
Holding company, estate tax payments,
  106–107
Hope Scholarship credit, 14–15, 72–73,
  75–79

Income deferral, 27
Income tax liability, distribution of:
  distributional effects of Conference
    Agreement for H.R. 1836, 190–195
  estimated budget effects of
    Conference Agreement for H.R.
    1836, 196–219
  2001, 188–189
Individual retirement accounts (IRAs):
  catch-up contributions, 119–120
  contribution limits, 9–10, 64,
    115–117, 129
  deductible contributions, 115–117
  deemed, 121–122
  distributions, 13, 145–147
  employer plans, 13, 121–122
  mandatory distributions, automatic
    rollovers, 149–150
  matched contributions, 13
  minimum distribution rules, 136–137
  nonrefundable credit for
    contributions, 128–131

payroll-deduction arrangements,
    168–169
  rollover, 13, 145–147
  60-day rule, waiver of, 147–148
  types of, *see specific types of IRAs*
  vesting schedules, 13
  withdrawal tax, 119
Inflation, impact of, 5, 7–8, 12, 27, 31,
    57, 96–97, 137–138, 169
Inherited property, stepped-up basis:
  eligible property, 97, 99
  ineligible property, 98–99
  overview, 16, 93, 95–98, 106,
    109–110
Interest, as disqualified income, 54
Internal Revenue Code, 121–122, 142,
    156
Internal Revenue Service (IRS):
  early retirement benefits, 153
  installment agreements, 18
  IRA rollover waiver, 13, 147–148
  rebate checks, 17–18
  special needs beneficiary, defined,
    65–66
  transfer of property, 103
  user fees, elimination for certain
    determination letter requests
    regarding employer plans, 166–167
  wage withholding tables, 23
IRS Form 8812, 40
Itemized deductions:
  charitable contributions, 27
  limitations on, 31–33
  restrictions on, 6

Joint life and last survivor expectancy,
    136
Joint returns:
  alternative minimum tax (AMT)
    exemption, 6, 36–37
  earned income credit, 59
  education tax breaks, 13–15
  15 percent tax bracket, 51–53
  IRA contribution limitations, 117, 129
  marriage penalty, 7
  personal exemption, 34
  rebate checks, 29
  standard deduction, 51–52
  tax brackets, 2–3

Joint returns (*Continued*)
  tax rate reductions, 5, 22, 26
  tax rate schedules for 2001, 25
  10 percent bracket income levels, 23

Lifetime Learning credit, 14–15, 72–73,
  75–80
Local government employees, 137, 141,
  157
Low-income workers:
  earned income credit, 53
  retirement savings tax credit, 12

Marriage bonus, 49
Marriage penalty relief:
  alternative minimum tax (AMT), 59
  delayed relief from, 6–7
  earned income credit, 53–59
  15 percent rate bracket for married
    couples filing jointly, 50–53
  overview, 49–50
  standard deduction, 50–51
Married couples filing separately:
  alternative minimum tax (AMT)
    exemption, 6, 36–37
  college education deduction and, 72
  dependent care exclusion, 48
  earned income credit, 54, 59
  IRA contributions, 129
  personal exemption, 34
  rebate check, 3, 29
  tax rate reductions, 5, 22
  tax rate schedules for 2001, 25
  10 percent bracket income levels, 23
Medicare tax, 40
Military service, 60–day rule waiver,
  148
Minimum distribution rules:
  457 plans, 140–141
  403(b) annuities, 136–137
  IRAs, 136–137
Modified adjusted gross income
  (MAGI), in calculation of:
  adoption tax, 46
  child tax credit, 40
  college tuition deduction, 15
  earned income credit, 55–57
  education IRA income limitations,
    63–64

IRA contributions, 9–10, 129–130
  retirement savings tax credit, lower-
    income workers, 14–15
  Roth IRA contributions, 118
  student loan interest deduction, 14,
    81
Money purchase pension plan, 155–156

Net capital gain income, 54
Net passive income, 54
Noncash assets, 103
Noncustodial parents, earned income
  credit, 59
Nondiscrimination rules, 10, 128, 134,
  160
Nonresidents who are not U.S.
  citizens, estate taxes, 97, 107–109
Nontaxable compensation, 55, 59

$1 million lifetime exclusion gift tax,
  15–16
Owner-employee(s):
  defined, 158
  plan loans for, 159
Ownership, closely held businesses,
  106

Partnerships:
  estate taxes, 106–107
  pension plan provisions, 158–159
  plan loans for, 158–159
Penalties:
  for improper reporting of gifts,
    103–104
  marriage, *see* Marriage penalty relief
Pension plans, *see specific types of
  pension plans*
  benefit limits, 121–123
  cash-out rules, 173–174
  compensation limits, 123–124
  contribution limits, 11–12, 120–123
  coordination requirements for
    deferred compensation plans of
    state and local governments and
    tax-exempt organizations, 164–166
  deduction limitations for employers,
    157–158
  deferrals for employees age 50 or
    older, 130–132

defined contribution plans,
   employee contributions, 169–170
distributions, 151–153, 170–173
domestic employees, 144–145
elective deferral limitations,
   124–125, 163–164
employer-provided retirement
   advice, treatment of, 176–177
employer-related changes, 155–158
hardship withdrawal provisions,
   142–144
IRS user fees, elimination for certain
   determination letter requests
   regarding employer plans, 166–167
minimum distribution rules, 136–137
nonrefundable credit for elective
   deferrals and IRA contributions,
   128–130
partnership provisions, 158–159
reduction in plan benefits, 155–156
rollovers, 145–148
salary reduction catch-up
   contributions, 130–134
S corporation provisions, 158–159
60-day waiver of rollover, 147–148
small business tax credit for new
   retirement plan expenses,
   168–169
sole proprietorship provisions,
   158–159
top-heavy, 159–163
vesting, of employer matching
   contributions, 134–136
Personal exemption restriction, 6, 27,
   33–35
Plan administrator, function of, 156
Prepaid tuition programs, 14, 67–68
Present value, 154
Principal residence, sale of, *see* Sale or
   exchange of principal residence
Profit sharing plans, 12, 158

Qualified domestic relations order
   (QDRO), 139–140, 156
Qualified retirement plans, accrued
   benefit amendment, 151–152
Qualified state tuition plans (QSTPs),
   66, 68, 73
Qualified trusts, 60

Qualified tuition plan (QTP), *see*
   Section 529 qualified tuition plans
contributions to, 78–80
distributions, 68–70, 78–79
private college plan, 67–68
rollover options, 69–70
withdrawal penalties, 69
Qualifying child, for earned income
   credit, 54–55, 57–59

Real estate, sale of, 60. *See also* Sale or
   exchange of principal residence
Rebate checks:
calculation of, 3–4, 29
eligibility for, 18, 29–30
maximum amounts, 18, 29–30
purpose of, 3, 23
state taxes, effect on, 18–19
tax credits distinguished from, 2–3
tax liability, effect on, 27
timing of, 2–3, 17–19
Relationship test, qualifying children,
   54–55, 57–59
Rental income, 54
Reporting requirements, estate taxes,
   102–103
Retirement age, 122–123
Retirement planning, employer-
   provided, 176–177
Retirement savings tax credit, 12
Revocable trusts, 60
Rollover/rollover distributions:
automatic mandatory, 149–150
cash-out rules, 173–174
eligible rollover distribution,
   defined, 145
hardship withdrawals and, 143
opportunities for, 13
pension plans, 145–147
tax consequences of, 150–151
Roth IRA:
contribution limits, 9, 12, 64,
   118–119, 129
deemed, 121
early distributions, 119
elective deferrals, 11, 126–128
nondeductible contributions, 126
tax-free distributions, 11, 126
traditional IRA conversion to, 126

Roth IRA (*Continued*)
  withdrawal restrictions, 118, 126
  withdrawal tax, 118
Royalty income, 54

Safe harbor rules, 142
Salary reduction, catch-up
    contributions, 131–134
Sale or exchange of principal
    residence, estate taxes, 60, 100–102
Same-desk rule, 171
Scholarships, *see* Hope Scholarship
    credit
  under National Health Service Corps
    and Armed Forces Health
    Professions programs, 82–83
  tax-free, 79
S corporations, pension plan
    provisions, 158–159
Section 529 qualified tuition plans:
  benefits of, generally, 14
  contributions, increase in, 61
  distributions, 67–69, 73
  private college plans, 67–68
  rollover option, 67, 69–70
  types of plans, 66–67
Section 204(h) notice, 155–156
Self-employment, generally:
  fee, 27
  tax, 40
Separation from service, 170–171
SIMPLE plans:
  contributions to, 12, 129, 144–145
  domestic employees, 144–145
  elective deferrals, 10–11, 124–125,
    131–133, 164–165
  new retirement plan expenses, tax
    credit for, 168
Simplified employee pension (SEP)
    plans:
  contributions, 12, 129
  elective deferrals, 10–11, 124–125,
    131–133, 164–165
  new retirement plan expenses, tax
    credit for, 168–169
Single filers:
  alternative minimum tax (AMT)
    exemption, 6, 36–37
  education tax breaks, 13–15

IRA contribution limitations, 116,
    129
  personal exemption, 34
  rebate check maximum, 29
  standard deduction, 51
  tax rate reductions, 5, 22, 26
  tax rate schedules for 2001, 25
  10 percent bracket income levels, 23
Single-sum distribution, 153, 155
60-day waiver for IRA rollover, 13,
    147–148
Small business tax credit, new
    retirement plan expenses, 168–169
Social Security:
  retirement age, 122
  tax, 40, 42
Sole proprietorship, pension plan
    provisions, 158–159
Special needs beneficiary, 65
Special needs children:
  adoptions, 8–9, 43–45
  Education IRAs for, 65–66
Standard deduction, 7, 50–51
State death tax:
  credit, 16–17, 91–92
  defined, 93
State government employees, 137, 141,
    157
State taxes, tax rebate effects, 18–19
Stepchildren, tax treatment of, 54,
    57–58
Stepped-up basis, 15–16, 93–99
    105–106, 109
Stock bonus plans, 12, 158
Student loan interest deduction, 14–15,
    81–82
Subsidiaries, employment with, 172
Support test, 55
Surviving spouse:
  alternative minimum tax (AMT)
    exemption, 36–37
  estate taxes, 16, 97–99
  rollover distributions, 146
Survivor annuities, 153, 155

Tax brackets, *see* Tax rate reductions
  federal, history of, 185–187
  projected, for 2006, 28
  types of, *see specific tax brackets*

Tax credits, 2–3. *See also types of credits*
Tax-exempt organizations, 64, 137, 141, 157
Taxpayer Relief Act of 1997, 39, 175
Tax planning, 27
Tax rate reductions:
  gift tax, 15–16, 86, 90
  individual income tax structure, 21
  inflation adjustments, 27
  phased-in, 4–5, 22–23
  prior-law tax rates, 22
  projected income tax brackets for 2006, 28
  regular income schedules, 24–25
  small, for 2001, 4
  unified estate and gift tax, 86–87
10 percent tax bracket, 2–4, 23
35 percent tax bracket, 23
33 percent tax bracket, 23
Top-heavy plans:
  defined, 159–160
  determination date, 160
  key employee, defined, 160–161
  nonkey employees, minimum benefit for, 161–163
  qualification requirements, 159
Trade and business expenses, 145
Transfer of property, 16. *See also* Sale or exchange of principal residence

Transfer of stock, 98, 100
Treasury Department, 2, 4
28 percent tax bracket, 23
25 percent tax bracket, 23

Unified credit, estate taxes:
  defined, 87
  tax rates and, 88–90

Vesting schedule, of employer matching contributions, 13, 134–136

Wage withholding tables, revised, 4, 23
Waiver, IRA rollovers, 13, 147–148
Widow(er)s, *see* Surviving spouse
  alternative minimum tax (AMT) exemption, 6, 36–37
  tax brackets, 3
  tax rate schedules for 2001, 25
Withdrawal, generally:
  hardship, 142–144
  qualified tuition plans (QTPs), 69
  restrictions for traditional IRAs, 117
  Roth IRAs, 118, 126
  tax, 118–119
Women, elective deferral provisions for, 131
Working-condition fringe benefits, 176

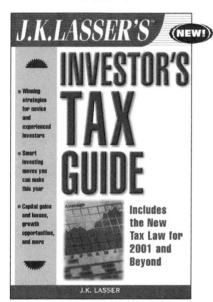